JESUS
THE WAY, THE

A daily prayer book

David Konstant

McCrimmons
Great Wakering, Essex

First published in United Kingdom in 1981
by Collins Liturgical Publications

This edition (revised) published in United Kingdom in 2001
by MCCRIMMON PUBLISHING CO. LTD.
10-12 High Street, Great Wakering, Essex, SS3 0EQ
Email: mccrimmons@dial.pipex.com
Website: www.mccrimmons.com

ISBN 0 85597 634 9

British Library Cataloguing in Publication Data.
A catalogue record for this book is available from the British Library.

Acknowledgements – (see page 200)

Illustrations by The Benedictine Sisters of Turvey Abbey

Way of the Cross pictures on pages 153-182 are taken from the wood scuptures
by Eric Gill and used by kind permission of Westminster Cathedral

Cover and layout by Nick Snode
Body text set in Clearface Regular 11pt and Baker Signet BT 12pt
Heading set in Baker Signet BT 36pt and 28pt
Printed and bound by Thanet Press Ltd., Margate, Kent

CONTENTS

Preface 5

Introduction 7

Morning Prayer 11

Jesus Christ, the Way 17

Jesus Christ, the Truth 41

Jesus Christ, the Life 61

Jubilee 89

A Meditation on the
     Mysteries of the Rosary 99

A Meditation on the Beatitudes 133

A Meditation on the Way of the Cross . . 153

An Examination of Conscience 183

Night Prayer 191

Index 195

PREFACE

THE spire at Salisbury Cathedral is one of the finest in the world. It is a surprise to learn that the original wooden scaffolding is still inside it. Although it is no longer needed it has somehow become a part of the spire. A prayer book like this is a little like the scaffolding. It is a skeleton around which you can build your own prayers. To begin with the prayers are someone else's but as you repeat them they become truly your own and may provide small beginnings for your own conversations with God.

When Jesus began his public ministry he quoted a passage from Isaiah: "The spirit of the Lord God is upon me, because the Lord has anointed me; he has sent me to bring good news to the oppressed, to bind up the brokenhearted, to proclaim liberty to the captives, and release to the prisoners; to proclaim the year of the Lord's favour." (61:1-2). Then he said: "Today this scripture has been fulfilled in your hearing" (Luke 4:21). The Good News was his Jubilee message. The message is that God's promises to us are even now being fulfilled through Jesus Christ—through all he said and did. That is why Jesus is truly and uniquely the Way, the Truth and the Life (see John 14:6).

The evangelists have written down their accounts of the Good News so that we might grasp it and make it our own. They help us on our journey with Jesus Christ and our fellow pilgrims as we discover and come to believe how wonderful the good news is, and so begin to write our own good news, our own gospel.

This prayer book begins with a brief morning prayer. There is then a reflection on Jesus Christ: the Way, the Truth and the Life, as portrayed in the Gospels themselves, as exemplified in other passages of Scripture, and also as reflected by Christian writers. This part concludes with a focus on aspects of the

Great Jubilee, so as to mark the new Millennium. The second principal part of the book highlights certain aspects of Jesus's life and preaching, through scripturally based meditations on the Rosary, the Beatitudes and the Way of the Cross. There is then an invitation to look honestly at ourselves and to make an examination of conscience, perhaps as a preparation for celebrating our forgiveness by God in the Sacrament of Penance. The prayer book concludes with a suggestion for night prayer.

I hope that this small scaffolding of prayer will help you to write your own gospel, as you discover how rich is the good news God has brought you. A cathedral spire, however beautiful, cannot reach heaven. But the building you make by your prayer is one where God truly dwells.

DAVID KONSTANT
July 2001

INTRODUCTION

The apostles watched Jesus praying and were so moved by what they saw that they said: 'Lord, teach us to pray.'

He said to them,
"When you pray, say:
Father, hallowed be your name.
Your kingdom come.
Give us each day our daily bread.
And forgive us our sins,
for we ourselves forgive everyone
indebted to us.
And do not bring us to the time of trial."

Luke 11:2-4

JESUS urged his friends to pray: in the privacy of their rooms; together, where a few were assembled in his name; without babbling, but urgently, insistently, with confidence and joy, generously, openly, hopefully, always giving praise to God, and always listening to him. We are his friends, and so we too pray, each in our own way.

Sometimes we may feel the urge to express our prayer in words; at other times we may find that by repeating a word or phrase (like, 'Come, Lord Jesus') we are soon absorbed in God's presence; or perhaps it will be enough for us on occasion to be quite still and know that God enfolds us.

Words, though, are almost always the beginning of our daily prayer. So here are some words that may help us to find God. They are pointers to prayer. Some are the words of the Old Testament psalmist; some are Jesus's own words; some are from the early followers of Jesus; there are prayers hallowed by the Church; and there are words of ordinary people, who in their own way have spoken to God. If they help us in our turn to find God at odd moments of the day, these words have done their work and will not return to him empty handed.

God approaches us through all our senses. So there are many things apart from words that may lead us to prayer. Music, beauty, even something as indefinable as atmosphere, can help us raise our minds and hearts to God. There are a number of illustrations in the book to provoke us to prayer, to accompany the written word, or perhaps to stand on their own as a silent meditation on God's work.

The pattern of this book of prayers is Jesus Christ: the Way, the Truth, the Life—a description Jesus gave of himself that inspires unending reflection. He said: 'I am the Way, the Truth and the Life. No one can come to the Father except through me.' (John 14:6)

Here are three prayers that offer some thoughts for reflection.

> Come, my Way, my Truth, my Life:
> Such a Way as gives us breath:
> Such a Truth as ends all strife:
> Such a Life as killeth death.
>
> *George Herbert*

> O Lord Jesus Christ, who art the Way, the Truth, and the Life, we pray thee suffer us not to stray from thee who art the Way, nor to distrust thee who art the Truth, nor to rest in any other thing than thee, who art the Life. Teach us by thy Holy Spirit what to believe, what to do and wherein to take our rest. Amen.
>
> *Erasmus*

Lord Jesus Christ, Son of the living God,
teach us to walk in your Way more trustfully,
to accept your Truth more faithfully,
and to share your Life more lovingly.
By the power of the Holy Spirit
help us in our work for the Church
so that we may come as one family
to the kingdom of the Father,
where you live for ever and ever. Amen.

Prayer for the National Pastoral Congress (1980)

We begin our day remembering God's continual presence (our morning prayer), and we end the day trustfully, putting ourselves in his hands (our evening prayer). In between times, alone or with others, we may turn to him in adoration, in praise, as petitioners, as sorrowful sinners. Always we may be sure that God hears and answers our prayers.

Morning Prayer

I F WE are to remain close to God as to a friend, we need, at certain times of the day, to greet him and to listen to him. When we wake in the morning, and before we go to sleep at night, are good moments to place ourselves in his presence and to be still with him.

  ## THE SIGN OF THE CROSS

  In the name of the Father,
and of the Son,
and of the Holy Spirit. Amen.

Remember that God is present.

> I call upon you, for you will answer me, O God;
> incline your ear to me, hear my words.

Psalm 17:6

Pause for a moment's silent prayer of adoration.

A PRAYER OF PRAISE AND THANKS

O LORD, OUR SOVEREIGN, how majestic is your name in all the earth!

You have set your glory above the heavens. Out of the mouths of babes and infants you have founded a bulwark because of your foes, to silence the enemy and the avenger.

When I look at your heavens, the work of your fingers,
the moon and the stars that you have established;
what are human beings that you are mindful of them,
mortals that you care for them?

Yet you have made them a little lower than God,
and crowned them with glory and honour.
You have given them dominion over the works of your
    hands;
you have put all things under their feet,
all sheep and oxen, and also the beasts of the field,
the birds of the air, and the fish of the sea,
whatever passes along the paths of the seas.

O LORD, our Sovereign, how majestic is your name in all
the earth!

Psalm 8

*The apostles asked Jesus to teach them to pray; he teaches us
the same prayer to God who is our Father:*

Our Father, who art in heaven,
hallowed be thy name;
thy kingdom come;
thy will be done on earth as it is in heaven.
Give us this day our daily bread;
and forgive us our trespasses
as we forgive those who trespass against us;
and lead us not into temptation,
but deliver us from evil. Amen.

*Pause for a moment's silent reflection; remember those
whose forgiveness we need, and those whom we must forgive;
remember the blessings that are our daily bread – family,
friends, work, leisure, home, happiness – and thank God;
remember the hardships, sorrows and temptations of daily
life, and pray for strength and perseverance.*

A PRAYER OF SELF-GIVING
FOR THE DAY'S WORK

Lord God,
you have brought me to a new day.
Give me grace today to work for your glory,
and for my neighbour's good;
so that all I say and do,
and think and pray,
may make this day a perfect gift.
    Amen.

A PRAYER OF CONFIDENCE TO THE GOD
WHO ALWAYS CARES

The LORD is my shepherd,
I shall not want.
He makes me lie down in green pastures;
he leads me beside still waters;
he restores my soul.

He leads me in right paths
for his name's sake.
Even though I walk through the darkest valley,
I fear no evil;
for you are with me; your rod and your staff
– they comfort me.

You prepare a table before me
in the presence of my enemies;
you anoint my head with oil;
my cup overflows.

Surely goodness and mercy shall follow me
all the days of my life,
and I shall dwell in the house of the LORD
my whole life long.

Psalm 23

SOME PRAYERS FOR THE DAY

I praise and thank you, Lord, for your goodness
    to me.
Stay always close to me.

Lord, you know me through and through.
Forgive my sins;
give me the grace to choose the better way.

Lord, I believe in you;
increase my faith.

Lord, I hope in you;
be a friend to me.

Lord, I love you,
show me how to live.

*We may pause now to pray for those we love and those who
are in need.*
*Remember that we belong to the whole family of God, and
ask all the saints to pray for us and with us. Mary is the first
of all the saints and so we pray:*

Hail Mary, full of grace, the LORD is with thee.
Blessed art thou among women,
and blessed is the fruit of thy womb, Jesus.
Holy Mary, mother of God, pray for us sinners
now and at the hour of our death. Amen.

*Finally, as we begin the day's work, we may praise God again
in the words of a familiar prayer:*

 Glory be to the Father,
and to the Son,
and to the Holy Spirit;
as it was in the beginning
is now and ever shall be,
world without end. Amen.

Jesus Christ, the Way

Our steps are made firm by the LORD,
when he delights in our way;
though we stumble, we shall not fall headlong,
for the LORD holds us by the hand.

Psalm 37:23-24

JESUS invites us, like the apostles, to listen to his call and to follow him; to be his disciples; to learn that leadership demands service; to walk the way of self-denial, of poverty and of obedience; to come to him in our sickness, our anger and our sinfulness; to pray; to be unworried; to work confidently and to live peaceably in our homes so as to be happy with him for ever.

VOCATION

G OD has created me to do him some definite service. He has committed some work to me which he has not committed to another. I have my mission – I may never know it in this life, but I shall be told it in the next.

I am a link in a chain, a bond of connexion between persons. He has not created me for naught. I shall do good, I shall do his work. I shall be an angel of peace, a preacher of truth in my own place while not intending it – if I do but keep his commandments.

Therefore I will trust him. Whatever, wherever I am. I can never be thrown away. If I am in sickness, my sickness may serve him; in perplexity, my perplexity may serve him; if I am in sorrow, my sorrow may serve him. He does nothing in vain. He knows what he is about. He may take away my friends, he may throw me among strangers. He may make me feel desolate, make my spirits sink, hide my future from me – still he knows what he is about.

Cardinal Newman

 Lord, give courage and strength to the young. Help them to choose their work and make the right decisions for their way of life.

Bidding Prayer

THEREFORE, BROTHERS AND SISTERS, be all the more eager to confirm your call and election, for if you do this, you will never stumble. For in this way, entry into the eternal kingdom of our Lord and Saviour Jesus Christ will be richly provided for you

2 Peter 1:10-11

We have been enlightened by Christ.
We are to walk always as children of the light.
May we keep the flame of faith alive in our
    hearts.
When the Lord comes,
may he go out to meet us with all the saints
in the heavenly kingdom.

From the Baptismal Service

DISCIPLESHIP

Christ be near at either hand,
Christ behind, before me stand,
Christ with me where e'er I go,
Christ around, above, below.

Christ be in my heart and mind,
Christ within my soul enshrined,
Christ control my wayward heart:
Christ abide and ne'er depart.

Christ my life and only Way.
Christ my lantern night and day;
Christ be my unchanging friend,
Guide and Shepherd to the end.

tr. J Fennelly

THUS SAYS THE LORD: Stand at the crossroads, and look, and ask for the ancient paths, where the good way lies; and walk in it, and find rest for your souls.

Jeremiah 6:16

THEREFORE PREPARE YOUR MINDS for action; discipline yourselves; set all your hope on the grace that Jesus Christ will bring you when he is revealed. Like obedient children, do not be conformed to the desires that you formerly had in ignorance. Instead, as he who called you is holy, be holy yourselves in all your conduct; for it is written, "You shall be holy, for I am holy."

1 Peter 1:13-16

AS HE WAS WALKING ALONG, he saw Levi son of Alphaeus sitting at the tax booth, and he said to him, "Follow me." And he got up and followed him.

Mark 2:14

ANOTHER SAID, "I WILL FOLLOW YOU, LORD; but let me first say farewell to those at my home." Jesus said to him, "No one who puts a hand to the plough and looks back is fit for the kingdom of God."

Luke 9:61-62

PETER BEGAN TO SAY TO HIM, "Look, we have left everything and followed you." Jesus said, "Truly I tell you, there is no one who has left house or brothers or sisters or mother or father or children or fields, for my sake and for the sake of the good news, who will not receive a hundredfold now in this age— houses, brothers and sisters, mothers and children, and fields with persecutions—and in the age to come eternal life."

Mark 10:28-30

COME TO ME, all you that are weary and are carrying heavy burdens, and I will give you rest. Take my yoke upon you, and learn from me; for I am gentle and humble in heart, and you will find rest for your souls. For my yoke is easy, and my burden is light.

Matthew 11:28-30

A DISCIPLE IS NOT ABOVE THE TEACHER, nor a slave above the master; it is enough for the disciple to be like the teacher, and the slave like the master.

Matthew 10:24-25

LET THE SAME MIND BE IN YOU that was in Christ Jesus.

Philippians 2:5

Lord, I give you today my prayers, thoughts, works, sufferings and joys, that they may be for your glory and for the good of the world.

A Morning Offering

Jesu, blessed Jesu, strengthen me in soul and body, that I may not fail you.

St John Paine

AGAIN JESUS SPOKE to them, saying,
"I am the light of the world. Whoever follows me will never walk in darkness but will have the light of life."

John 8:12

Lord Jesus,
I give you my hands to do your work.
I give you my feet to go your way.
I give you my eyes to see as you do.
I give you my tongue to speak your words.
I give you my mind that you may think in me.
I give you my spirit that you may pray in me.
Above all, I give you my heart
that you may love in me your Father and all mankind.
I give you my whole self that you may grow in me,
so that it is you, Lord Jesus,
who live and work and pray in me.

Grail Prayer

LEADERSHIP

THE GREATEST AMONG YOU will be your servant. All who exalt themselves will be humbled, and all who humble themselves will be exalted

Matthew 23:11-12

WHOEVER WISHES TO BE FIRST among you must be slave of all. For the Son of Man came not to be served but to serve, and to give his life a ransom for many.

Mark 10:44-45

THE LORD YOUR GOD carried you, just as one carries a child, all the way that you travelled until you reached this place

Deuteronomy 1:31

SINCE, THEN, WE HAVE A GREAT HIGH PRIEST who has passed through the heavens, Jesus, the Son of God, let us hold fast to our confession. For we do not have a high priest who is unable to sympathize with our weaknesses, but we have one who in every respect has been tested as we are, yet without sin. Let us therefore approach the throne of grace with boldness, so that we may receive mercy and find grace to help in time of need.

Hebrews 4:15-16

I LED THEM WITH CORDS OF HUMAN KINDNESS, with bands of love. I was to them like those who lift infants to their cheeks. I bent down to them and fed them

Hosea 11:3

THEREFORE, since we are surrounded by so great a cloud of witnesses, let us also lay aside every weight and the sin that clings so closely, and let us run with perseverance the race that is set before us, looking to Jesus the pioneer and perfecter of our faith, who for the sake of the joy that was set before him endured the cross, disregarding its shame, and has taken his seat at the right hand of the throne of God.

Hebrew 12:2

SERVICE

Teach us, good Lord,
to serve you as you deserve;
to give and not to count the cost,
to fight and not to heed the wounds,
to toil and not to seek for rest,
to labour and not to ask for any reward,
save that of knowing that we do your will;
through Jesus Christ our Lord. Amen.

St Ignatius

SO NOW, O ISRAEL, what does the LORD your God require of you? Only to fear the LORD your God, to walk in all his ways, to love him, to serve the LORD your God with all your heart and with all your soul.

Deuteronomy 10:12

DO NOT REPAY ANYONE EVIL FOR EVIL. If your enemies are hungry, feed them. Do not be overcome by evil, but overcome evil with good.

from Romans 12:17-21

I was hungry and you gave me food.
   Blessed be God for ever.
I was thirsty and you gave me drink.
   Blessed be God for ever.
I was a stranger and you made me welcome.
   Blessed be God for ever.
I was naked and you clothed me.
   Blessed be God for ever.
I was sick and you visited me.
   Blessed be God for ever.
I was in prison and you came to see me.
   Blessed be God for ever.

from Matthew 25

NOW THERE ARE VARIETIES OF GIFTS, but the same Spirit; and there are varieties of services, but the same Lord; and there are varieties of activities, but it is the same God who activates all of them in everyone. To each is given the manifestation of the Spirit for the common good.

1 Corinthians 12:4-6

THE GREATEST AMONG YOU must become like the youngest, and the leader among you like one who serves. For who is the greater, the one who is at the table or the one who serves? Is it not the one at the table? But I am among you as one who serves.

Luke 22:27

VERY TRULY, I TELL YOU, servants are not greater than their master, nor are messengers greater than the one who sent them.

John 13:16

LIKE GOOD STEWARDS of the manifold grace of God, serve one another with whatever gift each of you has received. Whoever speaks must do so as one speaking the very words of God; whoever serves must do so with the strength that God supplies, so that God may be glorified in all things through Jesus Christ. To him belong the glory and the power forever and ever. Amen.

1 Peter 4:10-11

 Make us worthy, Lord,
to serve our brothers and sisters
throughout the world,
who live and die in poverty and hunger.
Give them by our hands
this day their daily bread,
and by our understanding love
give peace and joy.

Thomas Cullinan OSB

SELF-DENIAL

THEN JESUS TOLD HIS DISCIPLES, "If any want to become my followers, let them deny themselves and take up their cross and follow me. For those who want to save their life will lose it, and those who lose their life for my sake will find it. For what will it profit them if they gain the whole world but forfeit their life? Or what will they give in return for their life?"

Matthew 16:24-26

JESUS SAID:

"Very truly, I tell you, unless a grain of wheat falls into the earth and dies, it remains just a single grain; but if it dies, it bears much fruit."

John 12:24

HE HUMBLED HIMSELF and became obedient to the point of death—even death on a cross.

Philippians 2:8

'I AM NOW REJOICING in my sufferings for your sake, and in my flesh I am completing what is lacking in Christ's afflictions for the sake of his body, that is, the church.'

Colossians 1:24

> O blessed Jesu, make me understand and remember that whatsoever we gain, if we lose you, all is lost, and whatsoever we lose, if we gain you, all is gained.
>
> *St Thomas Cottam*

POVERTY

BLESSED are you who are poor,
    for yours is the kingdom of God.
Woe to you who are rich,
    for you have received your consolation.

Luke 6:20,24

GIVE SOME OF YOUR FOOD TO THE HUNGRY, and some of your clothing to the naked. Give all your surplus as alms, and do not let your eye begrudge your giving of alms.

Tobit 4:16-17

EVERYONE WHO THIRSTS, come to the waters;
    and you that have no money, come, buy and eat!
Come, buy wine and milk
    without money and without price.

Isaiah 55:1

O Lord Jesus Christ, take as your right, receive as my gift, all my liberty, my memory, my understanding, my will; all that I have, all that I am, all that I can be. To you, O Lord, I restore it, all is yours, dispose of it according to your will. Give me your love. Give me your grace. It is enough for me.

St Ignatius

AS JESUS WAS SETTING OUT on a journey, a man ran up and knelt before him, and asked him, "Good Teacher, what must I do to inherit eternal life?" Jesus, looking at him, loved him and said, "You lack one thing; go, sell what you own, and give the money to the poor, and you will have treasure in heaven; then come, follow me." When he heard this, he was shocked and went away grieving, for he had many possessions.

from Mark 10:17-22

Two mites, two drops (yet all her house and land),
Falls from a steady heart, though trembling hand.
The other's wanton wealth foams high and brave,
The other cast away, she only gave.

Richard Crashaw

A CHEERFUL giver does not count the cost of what he gives. His heart is set on pleasing and cheering him to whom the gift is given.

Julian of Norwich

JESUS SAID TO HIS DISCIPLES, 'Truly I tell you, it will be hard for a rich person to enter the kingdom of heaven.'

Matthew 19:23

OBEDIENCE

We should rather love obedience than fear disobedience.

St Francis de Sales

NOW THAT YOU HAVE PURIFIED YOUR SOULS by your obedience to the truth so that you have genuine mutual love, love one another deeply from the heart. You have been born anew, not of perishable but of imperishable seed, through the living and enduring word of God. For [as scripture says]
   "All flesh is like grass and all its glory like the flower of grass. The grass withers, and the flower falls, but the word of the Lord endures forever."
That word is the good news that was announced to you.

1 Peter 1:22-25

 Almighty, ever-living God,
make us ever obey you willingly and promptly.
Teach us how to serve you
with sincere and upright hearts
in every sphere of life.

The Prayer of the Church

BE STRONG, BE COURAGEOUS, and keep the charge of the Lord your God, walking in his ways and keeping his statutes, his commandments, his ordinances, and his testimonies, so that you may prosper in all that you do and wherever you turn.

1 Kings 2:2-3

NO MAN SECURELY COMMANDS but he who has learned to obey.

Thomas à Kempis

NOW MAY THE GOD OF PEACE, who brought back from the dead our Lord Jesus, make you complete in everything good so that you may do his will, working among us that which is pleasing in his sight.

Hebrews 13:20-21

NOT EVERYONE who says to me, "Lord, Lord," will enter the kingdom of heaven, but only the one who does the will of my Father in heaven.

Matthew 7:21

JESUS SAID TO THEM,
   "My food is to do the will of him who sent me
   and to complete his work."

John 4:34

ANGER

THE LORD PASSED BEFORE HIM, and proclaimed, "The LORD, the LORD, a God merciful and gracious, slow to anger, and abounding in steadfast love and faithfulness."

Exodus 34:6

   BLESSED ARE THE MEEK
   for they shall inherit the earth.

Matthew 5:4

LET NO EVIL TALK COME OUT OF YOUR MOUTHS, but only what is useful for building up, as there is need, so that your words may give grace to those who hear. And do not grieve the Holy Spirit of God, with which you were marked with a seal for the day of redemption. Put away from you all bitterness and wrath and anger and wrangling and slander, together with all malice, and be kind to one another, tender-hearted, forgiving one another, as God in Christ has forgiven you.

Ephesians 4:29-32

YOU MUST UNDERSTAND THIS, my beloved: let everyone be quick to listen, slow to speak, slow to anger; for your anger does not produce God's righteousness. If any think they are religious, and do not bridle their tongues but deceive their hearts, their religion is worthless.

James 1:19-20, 26

I SAW full surely that wherever our Lord appears, peace reigns, and anger has no place. For I saw no whit of anger in God.

Julian of Norwich

YET EVEN NOW, says the LORD,
return to me with all your heart…
Return to the LORD, your God,
for he is gracious and merciful,
slow to anger, and abounding in steadfast love,
and relents from punishing.

Joel 2:12-13

SORROW

YOU, O LORD, are a God merciful and gracious,
slow to anger and
abounding in steadfast love and faithfulness.
Turn to me and be gracious to me.

Psalm 85:15-16

A LEPER CAME TO HIM begging him, and kneeling he said to him, "If you choose, you can make me clean." Moved with pity, Jesus stretched out his hand and touched him, and said to him, "I do choose. Be made clean!" Immediately the leprosy left him, and he was made clean.

Mark 1:40-42

My God, I am sorry and ask forgiveness for my sins.
By the help of your grace I will try not to sin again.

An Act of Contrition.

NAKED I CAME from my mother's womb,
and naked shall I return there;
the LORD gave, and the LORD has taken away;
blessed be the name of the LORD.

Shall we receive the good at the hand of God,
and not receive the bad?

Job 1:21, 2:10

JESUS CHRIST, OUR SAVIOUR, you were like us in all things but sin. Be with me when I am tempted, and stay with me when I fall, so that by your grace I may learn to trust in your strength. Amen.

LORD JESUS CHRIST, Son of God
be merciful to me, a sinner.

cf. Luke 18:13

Almighty, ever-living God,
whose love surpasses all that we ask or deserve,
open up for us the treasures of your mercy.
Forgive us all that weighs on our conscience,
and grant us more even than we dare to ask.
We make our prayer through Christ our Lord. Amen.

A Sunday Prayer

 Lord God,
in your goodness have mercy on me:
do not look on my sins,
but take away my guilt.
Create in me a clean heart
and renew within me an upright spirit.

PRAYER

MY SOUL longs for you, O God.

see Psalm 42

FOR WHERE TWO OR THREE ARE GATHERED in my name,
I am there among them.

Matthew 18:20

To seek God
means first of all
to let yourself be found by him.
He is the God of Abraham, Isaac, and Jacob.
He is the God of Jesus Christ.
He is your God,
not because he is yours, but because you are his.

Rule for a New Brother

WHENEVER YOU PRAY, go into your room and shut the door and
pray to your Father who is in secret; and your Father who sees
in secret will reward you.

Matthew 6:6

AS A DEER LONGS for flowing streams
so my soul longs for you, O God.

Psalm 42:1

KEEP AWAKE AND PRAY that you may not come into the time of
trial; the spirit indeed is willing, but the flesh is weak.

Mark 14:38

ASK, AND IT WILL BE GIVEN YOU; search, and you will find;
knock, and the door will be opened for you. For everyone who
asks receives, and everyone who searches finds, and for
everyone who knocks, the door will be opened... If you then,
who are evil, know how to give good gifts to your children, how
much more will your Father in heaven give good things to
those who ask him!

Matthew 7:7-11

Who seeks to pray must first abandon life,
Acknowledging the sovereign source of good
That holds secure the world and all its strife,
Redeemed and saved by beckoning arms on wood.
In loss of self we find th'eternal One
Enfolding us in urgent, pulsing breath.
So we become a living soul, new won —
To be at one with him who conquered death.
Thus quickened by God's Spirit we can speak
As friend to friend in intimate appeal.
This presence found, naught else is there to seek;
Forgiveness reaped, no more is there to heal.
  Be still, absorbed, help firm in God's own hand,
  At peace with all who throng his welcoming land.

DK

MY EYES ARE AWAKE before each watch of the night,
that I may meditate on your promise.

Psalm 119:148

ASK AND YOU WILL RECEIVE, and so your joy may be complete.

John 16:24

 We fly to thy patronage,
O holy Mother of God.
Despise not our petitions in our necessities,
but deliver us always from all dangers,
O glorious and blessed virgin.

Traditional

I called with all my heart; Lord, hear me.

ANXIETY

ANSWER ME QUICKLY, O LORD;
my spirit fails.

Psalm 142:7

CAN A WOMAN FORGET her nursing child,
or show no compassion for the child of her womb?
Even these may forget,
yet I will not forget you
says the Lord God.

Isaiah 49:15

JESUS SAID: "Come to me, all you that are weary and are carrying heavy burdens, and I will give you rest. Take my yoke upon you, and learn from me; for I am gentle and humble in heart, and you will find rest for your souls. For my yoke is easy, and my burden is light."

Matthew 11:28-30

JESUS SAID TO HIS DISCIPLES: "Therefore I tell you, do not worry about your life, what you will eat, or about your body, what you will wear. For life is more than food, and the body more than clothing. Do not be afraid, little flock, for it is your Father's good pleasure to give you the kingdom."

Luke 12:22-23,32

BLESSED BE THE GOD AND FATHER of our Lord Jesus Christ, the Father of mercies and the God of all consolation, who consoles us in all our affliction, so that we may be able to console those who are in any affliction with the consolation with which we ourselves are consoled by God. For just as the sufferings of Christ are abundant for us, so also our consolation is abundant through Christ.

2 Corinthians 1:3-5

OUT OF MY DISTRESS I called on the LORD;
With the LORD on my side I do not fear.

Psalm 118:5-6

 Deliver us, Lord, from every evil,
and grant us peace in our day.
In your mercy keep us free from sin
and protect us from all anxiety
as we wait in joyful hope
for the coming of our Saviour, Jesus Christ.
Amen.

A Prayer before Communion

CHRIST HAS SAID, "My grace is sufficient for you, for power is made perfect in weakness." So, I will boast all the more gladly of my weaknesses, so that the power of Christ may dwell in me. Therefore I am content with weaknesses, insults, hardships, persecutions, and calamities for the sake of Christ; for whenever I am weak, then I am strong."

2 Corinthians 12:9-10

FAMILY

Guard your family, Lord, with constant loving care, for in your divine grace we place our only hope.

The Prayer of the Church

Lord, bless the household of which I form a part. Show us how we can help one another, share our interests and sorrows and joys with one another, be ready to make sacrifices for one another. I ask that I may find my joy in serving them as you found your joy in serving Mary and Joseph on earth.

Hubert van Zeller

AT THAT TIME JESUS SAID, "I thank you, Father, Lord of heaven and earth, because you have hidden these things from the wise and the intelligent and have revealed them to infants"

Matthew 11:25

JESUS SAID, "Truly I tell you, unless you change and become like children, you will never enter the kingdom of heaven. Whoever becomes humble like this child is the greatest in the kingdom of heaven."

Matthew 18:3-4

JESUS SAID: "Whoever welcomes one such child in my name welcomes me, and whoever welcomes me welcomes not me but the one who sent me."

Mark 9:37

A WIFE SHOULD REGARD HER HUSBAND as she regards Jesus Christ. Just as Christ is head of the Church and saves her, so is a husband the head of the family. A husband must love his wife just as Christ loved the Church and gave himself for her. Children have a duty to obey their parents. The commandment, 'Love your parents,' carries with it this promise, 'You will do well and live happily.' On their part, parents must never make their children resentful, but should bring them up, correct them, and guide them as the Lord does. Finally, grow strong in the Lord, with his strength. Pray all the time for whatever you need, under the guidance of the Holy Spirit.

from Ephesians 5 and 6

IF WE LOVE ONE ANOTHER,
God lives in us,
and his love is perfected in us.

1 John 4:12

I PRAY THAT, according to the riches of his glory, he may grant that you may be strengthened in your inner being with power through his Spirit, and that Christ may dwell in your hearts through faith, as you are being rooted and grounded in love. I pray that you may have the power to comprehend, with all the saints, what is the breadth and length and height and depth, and to know the love of Christ that surpasses knowledge, so that you may be filled with all the fullness of God.

Ephesians 3:16-19

THE DAY'S WORK

WHEN I LOOK AT YOUR HEAVENS,
    the work of your fingers,
    the moon and the stars that
        you have established;
what are human beings that
        you are mindful of them,
    mortals that you care for them?

Yet you have made them
        a little lower than God,
    and crowned them with glory
        and honour.
You have given them dominion
        over the works of your hands;
    you have put all things under their feet.
all sheep and oxen,
    and also the beasts of the field,
the birds of the air, and the fish of the sea,
    whatever passes along
        the paths of the seeas.

O LORD, our Sovereign,
    how majestic is your name
        in all the earth!   *Psalm 8:4-7*

DO NOT BE DECEIVED; God is not mocked, for you reap whatever you sow. If you sow to your own flesh, you will reap corruption from the flesh; but if you sow to the Spirit, you will reap eternal life from the Spirit. So let us not grow weary in doing what is right, for we will reap at harvest-time, if we do not give up. So then, whenever we have an opportunity, let us work for the good of all, and especially for those of the family of faith.

Galatians 6:7-10

WE APPEAL TO YOU, brothers and sisters, to respect those who labour among you, and have charge of you in the Lord and admonish you; esteem them very highly in love because of their work. Be at peace among yourselves.

1 Thessalonians 5:12-13

Lord, be the beginning and end
of all that we do and say.
Prompt our actions with your grace
and complete them with your all-powerful help.
Through Christ our Lord. Amen.

A Sunday Prayer

Father, I dedicate this new day to you;
as I go about my work, I ask you to bless those I
    come into contact with.
Lord, I pray for all men and women who work to
    earn their living;
give them satisfaction in what they do.
Spirit of God, comfort the unemployed and their
    families;
they are your children and my brothers and sisters.
I ask you to help them find work soon.

A Morning Prayer

L AWFUL gain may and ought to be made of the business which you engage in; for without this, few men would be able to support themselves and their families, or do much good to others. But greediness after gain is a mischievous thing. 'They that will be rich fall into temptation and a snare, and into many foolish and hurtful lusts, which drown men in destruction and perdition; for the love of money is the root of all evil.' (1 Timothy 6:9-10) Among other qualifications of a righteous man this is one, that he 'despiseth the gain of oppressions' (Isaiah 33:15); that is to say, all gain but what is just and honest. Gain is a very strong temptation; against which, therefore, you must be upon your guard.

Rules for the Conduct of Life (Freeman of London)

God, Lord and Master of the vineyard,
you allot us our task,
and determine the just rewards of our labours.
Help us to bear the burden of the day
and accept your will in all things without
complaint.
Through Christ our Lord. Amen

The Prayer of the Church

Blessed are you, Lord God of all creation,
through your goodness we enjoy those things
that are the fruits of the earth and the work of
our hands,
may they be for us a source of lasting life.
Blessed be God for ever.

An Offertory Prayer

Jesus Christ, the Truth

In the beginning was the Word,
the Word was with God,
and the Word was God.

John 1:1

TRUTH is eternal and unchanging. 'Your truth, O Lord, will last from age to age.' Jesus promised to send his Spirit to lead us to all truth. This truth is the ground of our faith, the source of self-knowledge, the beginning of forgiveness and healing, the basis of justice and of peace; it is the cause of our joy; it is expressed in law; it is the only true foundation of unity.

SPIRIT

I WILL ASK THE FATHER,
and he will give you another Advocate,
to be with you forever.
This is the Spirit of truth.
The Advocate, the Holy Spirit,
whom the Father will send in my name,
will teach you everything,
and remind you of all that I have said to you.

John 14:16-17, 26

DO YOU NOT KNOW that your body is a temple of the Holy Spirit within you, which you have from God, and that you are not your own? For you were bought with a price; therefore glorify God in your body.

1 Corinthians 6:19-20

A NEW HEART I WILL GIVE YOU, and a new spirit I will put within you; and I will remove from your body the heart of stone and give you a heart of flesh. I will put my spirit within you, and make you follow my statutes and be careful to observe my ordinances, and you shall be my people, and I will be your God.

Ezekiel 36:25-26, 28

IN THE ONE SPIRIT we were all baptised into one body.

1 Corinthians 12:13

FOR ALL WHO ARE LED BY THE SPIRIT OF GOD are children of God. For you did not receive a spirit of slavery to fall back into fear, but you have received a spirit of adoption. When we cry, "Abba! Father!" it is that very Spirit bearing witness with our spirit that we are children of God, the Spirit helps us in our weakness; for we do not know how to pray as we ought, but that very Spirit intercedes with sighs too deep for words. And God, who searches the heart, knows what is the mind of the Spirit, because the Spirit intercedes for the saints according to the will of God.

Romans 8:14-16, 26-27

HOLY SPIRIT OF GOD, sent by the Father and the Son, fill my heart with your love. Lead me to know myself, to root out my selfishness, and to share with others the fruits of your presence: love, joy, peace, patience, kindness, generosity, faithfulness, gentleness and self-control.

cf. Galatians 5:22

FAITH

FOR GOD ALONE my soul waits in silence;
from him comes my salvation.
He alone is my rock and my salvation, my fortress;
I shall never be shaken.

Psalm 62:2-3

JESUS SAID:

"Truly I tell you, if you have faith the size of a mustard seed,
you will say to this mountain, 'Move from here to there,'
and it will move; and nothing will be impossible for you."

Matthew 17:20-21

JESUS SAID:

"I am the resurrection and the life.
Those who believe in me, even though they die, will live,
and everyone who lives and believes in me will never die.
Do you believe this?"

John 11:25-26

JESUS SAID TO THOMAS, "Put your finger here and see my hands. Reach out your hand and put it in my side. Do not doubt but believe." Thomas answered him, "My Lord and my God!" Jesus said to him, "Blessed are those who have not seen and yet have come to believe."

John 20:27-29

JESUS SAID:

> "Everyone therefore who acknowledges me before others, I also will acknowledge before my Father in heaven; but whoever denies me before others, I also will deny before my Father in heaven."
>
> *Matthew 10:32-33*

LORD I BELIEVE! Help my unbelief.

Mark 9:24

BY WHATEVER means he teaches us, his will is that we perceive him wisely, receive him joyfully, and keep ourselves in him faithfully.

Julian of Norwich

DISCIPLINE YOURSELVES, keep alert. Like a roaring lion your adversary the devil prowls around, looking for someone to devour. Resist him, steadfast in your faith, for you know that your brothers and sisters in all the world are undergoing the same kinds of suffering. And after you have suffered for a little while, the God of all grace, who has called you to his eternal glory in Christ, will himself restore, support, strengthen, and establish you. To him be the power forever and ever. Amen.

1 Peter 5:8-11

YOUR WORD IS A LAMP for my feet and a light for my path.

Psalm 119:105

IN OUR PRAYERS for you we always thank God, the Father of our Lord Jesus Christ, for we have heard of your faith in Christ Jesus and of the love that you have for all the saints, because of the hope laid up for you in heaven.

Colossians 1:3-4

O my God, I believe in you, and all that your Church teaches, because you have said it, and your word is true.

An Act of Faith

Lord God,
do not let false doctrine darken our minds,
since by the adoption of grace
you have made us children of light:
but grant that your light may shine within us
and we may always live in the brightness of truth.

A Sunday Prayer

FOR BY GRACE you have been saved through faith, and this is not your own doing; it is the gift of God – not the result of works, so that no one may boast. For we are what he has made us, created in Christ Jesus for good works, which God prepared beforehand to be our way of life.

Ephesians 2:8-10

I BELIEVE in God, the Father Almighty,
creator of heaven and earth;
and in Jesus Christ, his only Son, our Lord;
who was conceived by the Holy Spirit,
born of the Virgin Mary,
suffered under Pontius Pilate,
was crucified, died and was buried.
He descended into hell;
the third day he rose again from the dead.
He ascended into heaven
and sits at the right hand of God the almighty
    Father.
From thence he will come to judge the living and
    the dead.
I believe in the Holy Spirit;
the holy catholic Church;
the communion of saints;
the forgiveness of sins;
the resurrection of the body;
and the life everlasting. Amen

The Apostles' Creed

HUMILITY

IN THE SAME WAY, you who are younger must accept the authority of the elders. And all of you must clothe yourselves with humility in your dealings with one another, for "God opposes the proud, but gives grace to the humble." Humble yourselves therefore under the mighty hand of God, so that he may exalt you in due time.

1 Peter 5:5-6

> LET THE SAME MIND be in you that was in Christ Jesus,
> who, though he was in the form of God,
> did not regard equality with God
> as something to be exploited,
> but emptied himself,
> taking the form of a slave,
> being born in human likeness.
> And being found in human form,
> he humbled himself
> and became obedient to the point of death –
> even death on a cross.
> Therefore God also highly exalted him
> and gave him the name that is above every name,
> so that at the name of Jesus every knee should bend,
> in heaven and on earth and under the earth,
> and every tongue should confess that
> Jesus Christ is Lord, to the glory of God the Father.

Philippians 2:6-11

THE LORD LEADS THE HUMBLE in what is right,
and teaches the humble his way.

Psalm 25:9

UNLESS YOU CHANGE and become like children, you will never enter the kingdom of heaven.

Matthew 18:3

LEARN FROM ME; for I am gentle and humble in heart, and you will find rest for your souls.

Matthew 11:29

THE LORD does not see as mortals see; they look on the outward appearance, but the LORD looks on the heart.

from 1 Samuel 16:7

My soul glorifies the Lord,
my spirit rejoices in God, my saviour.
He looks on his servant in her lowliness;
henceforth all ages will call me blessed.

The Almighty works marvels for me.
Holy his name!
His mercy is from age to age,
on those who fear him.

He puts forth his arm in strength
and scatters the proud-hearted.
He casts the mighty from their thrones
and raises the lowly.

He fills the starving with good things,
and sends the rich away empty.

He protects Israel, his servant,
remembering his mercy,
the mercy promised to our fathers,
to Abraham and his sons for ever.

The Magnificat

The first degree of humility is obedience without delay.

St Benedict

IN all my walks it seems to me
that the grace of God lies in courtesy.

Hilaire Belloc

Almighty God, take from me all vainglorious
thoughts, all desires for mine own praise, all
envy, covetousness, gluttony, sloth and lechery,
all wrathful affections, all desire for revenge,
all delight in harm to others, all pleasure in provoking
them to wrath and anger, all delight in upbraiding and
insulting them in their affliction and calamity. Give
freely unto me, good Lord, thy love and favour which
my love for thee, be it ever so great, could not receive
except out of thine own great goodness.

St Thomas More

FORGIVENESS

Forgive us our trespasses,
as we forgive those who trespass against us.

The Our Father

JESUS SAID:

"For if you forgive others their trespasses, your heavenly
Father will also forgive you; but if you do not forgive others, neither will your Father forgive your trespasses."

Matthew 6:14-15

THEN PETER CAME AND SAID TO HIM, "Lord, if another member
of the church sins against me, how often should I forgive? As
many as seven times?" Jesus said to him, "Not seven times, but,
I tell you, seventy-seven times."

Matthew 18:21-22

JESUS SAID:

"Be merciful as your Father is merciful."

Luke 6:36

AS GOD'S CHOSEN ONES, holy and beloved, clothe yourselves with compassion, kindness, humility, meekness, and patience. Bear with one another and, if anyone has a complaint against another, forgive each other; just as the Lord has forgiven you, so you also must forgive. Above all, clothe yourselves with love, which binds everything together in perfect harmony. And let the peace of Christ rule in your hearts, to which indeed you were called in the one body. And be thankful.

Colossians 3:12-15

FATHER, FORGIVE THEM; for they do not know what they are doing.

Luke 23:34

 Give me thy grace, good Lord:
to set the world at nought,
to set my mind fast upon thee,
and not to hang upon the blast of men's mouths.
To be content to be solitary.
Not to long for worldly company.
Little and little utterly to cast off the world,
and rid my mind of all the business thereof.
Not to long to hear of any worldly things.
But that the hearing of worldly phantasies
may be to me displeasant.
Gladly to be thinking of God.
Piteously to call for his help.
To lean upon the comfort of God.
Busily to labour to love him.
To know mine own violence and wretchedness.
To humble myself under the mighty hand of God.
To bewail my sins past.
For the purging of them patiently to suffer
    adversity.
Gladly to bear my purgatory here.
To be joyful of tribulations.

St Thomas More

HEAL MY SOUL for I have sinned against you.

cf. Psalm 41:4

GRANT ME, O GOD, so worthily to receive this most holy body and blood of thy Son that I may thereby receive the forgiveness of all my sins, be filled with thy Holy Spirit, and find peace. For thou only art God and there is no other besides thee.

The Sarum Missal

To those who love you, Lord,
you promise to come with your Son
and make your home within them.
Come then with your purifying grace
and make our hearts a place where you can dwell.

A Sunday Prayer

Look in love on all whose sins have separated them from you. Reconcile them to yourself and to your Church.

Bidding Prayer

Cry wrenched wrung wounded radiant hearts,
    'O Christ, forgive!'
Beg nailed gnarled bloodied Christened hands,
    'Dear Jesu, bless!'
Smile blind burnt sunken glowing eyes,
    'Have mercy, Lord!'
Plead toiled torn aching tempered frames,
    'Sweet Master, save!'   *A Prayer of the Tortured (DK)*

Holy Father,
you know both our strength and our weakness.
Help us to know ourselves better
so that we will always judge ourselves
honestly and openly.
May we be guided by your Holy Spirit
who with you and your Son
is the source of all love and knowledge.

A Prayer for Confession

DO NOT BE WEARY in doing what is right.

2 Thessalonians 3:13

Enlighten our minds, O God, and purify our desires. Correct our wanderings and pardon our defects, so that by thy guidance we may be preserved from making shipwreck of our faith, be kept in a good conscience, and at length be landed in the safe haven of eternal peace. Through Jesus Christ our Lord. Amen.

St Anselm

HEALING

THE SON OF MAN came to seek out and to save the lost.

Luke 19:10

COME TO ME, all you that are weary and are carrying heavy burdens, and I will give you rest. Take my yoke upon you, and learn from me; for I am gentle and humble in heart, and you will find rest for your souls. For my yoke is easy, and my burden is light.

Matthew 11:28-30

THEREFORE, I TELL YOU, her sins, which were many, have been forgiven; hence she has shown great love. But the one to whom little is forgiven, loves little." Then he said to her, "Your sins are forgiven … Your faith has saved you; go in peace."

Luke 7:47-50

HELP US, O LORD OUR GOD, since we cannot flee from the body, or the body flee from us. We must needs carry about the body, because it is bound up with us. We cannot destroy it; we are forced to preserve it. But the world surrounds us and assails us through the five gateways of sense.

St Bernard

O LORD MY GOD, I cried to you for help and you have healed me.
I will give thanks to you for ever.

Psalm 30:3,13

Lord, support us as we pray,
protect us day and night,
so that we who under your guiding hand
live in a world of change,
may always draw strength from you,
with whom there is no shadow of alteration.

Evening Prayer

I LIFT UP MY EYES to the hills –
from where will my help come?
My help comes from the LORD,
who made heaven and earth.

Psalm 121:1-2

JUSTICE

RIGHTEOUSNESS AND JUSTICE are the foundation of your throne;
steadfast love and faithfulness go before you, O Lord.

Psalm 89:15

WHEN JESUS HEARD THIS, he said to the rich young man,
"There is still one thing lacking. Sell all that you own and
distribute the money to the poor, and you will have treasure in
heaven; then come, follow me." But when he heard this, he
became sad; for he was very rich.

Luke 18:22-23

BLESSED ARE THOSE WHO HUNGER and thirst for righteousness:
for they will be filled.

Matthew 5:6

Almighty Father, bring justice to our world, that your
people may live in the joy of your peace.

Bidding Prayer

WHAT DOES THE LORD REQUIRE OF YOU
but to do justice,
and to love kindness,
and to walk humbly with your God?

Micah 6:8

HOW DOES GOD'S LOVE ABIDE
in anyone who has the world's goods
and sees a brother or sister in need
and yet refuses help?
Little children,
let us love, not in word or speech,
but in truth and action.

1 John 3:17-18

YOU SHALL NOT BE INTIMIDATED by anyone, for the
judgment is God's.

Deuteronomy 1:17

Lord, make me an instrument of your peace:
Where there is hatred, let me sow love;
where there is injury, let me sow pardon;
where there is doubt, let me sow faith;
where there is despair, let me give hope;
where there is darkness, let me give light;
where there is sadness, let me give joy.

O Divine Master, grant that I may seek
    not to be comforted, but to comfort;
    not to be understood, but to understand;
    not to be loved, but to love.
Because it is in giving that we receive,
it is in forgiving that we are forgiven,
and it is in dying that we are born to eternal life.

att. to St Francis of Assisi

True Light of the World, Lord Jesus Christ,
as you enlighten all people for their salvation,
give us grace, we pray,
to herald your coming
by preparing the ways of justice and of peace.

Morning Prayer

PEACE

I HAVE CALMED AND QUIETED MY SOUL,
like a weaned child with its mother,
my soul is like the weaned child that is with me.

Psalm 131:2

NOW MAY THE LORD OF PEACE himself give you peace at all
times in all ways. The Lord be with all of you.

2 Thessalonians 3:16

BUT HE WAS WOUNDED for our transgressions,
crushed for our iniquities;
upon him was the punishment that made us whole,
and by his bruises we are healed.

Isaiah 53:5

I AM CONVINCED that neither death, nor life, nor angels, nor
rulers, nor things present, nor things to come, nor powers, nor
height, nor depth, nor anything else in all creation, will be able
to separate us from the love of God in Christ Jesus our Lord.

Romans 8:39

JESUS CAME AND STOOD AMONG THE DISCIPLES and said, "Peace
be with you." After he said this, he showed them his hands and
his side. Then the disciples rejoiced when they saw the Lord.
Jesus said to them again, "Peace be with you. As the Father has
sent me, so I send you."

John 20:20-21

Lord Jesus Christ, you said to your apostles:
"I leave you peace, my peace I give you."
Look not on our sins, but on the faith of your Church,
and grant us the peace and unity of your kingdom
where you live for ever and ever. Amen.

A Prayer before Communion

Guide our steps, good Lord, in the ways of your service,
and forgive us our sins, that we may discover the gift of
your peace and share it with others.

The Prayer of the Church

BLESSED ARE THE PEACEMAKERS, for they will be called
children of God.

Matthew 6:9

 Deep peace of the running wave to you.
Deep peace of the flowing air to you.
Deep peace of the quiet earth to you.
Deep peace of the shining stars to you.
Deep peace of the Son of Peace to you.

Irish Blessing

DO NOT WORRY about anything, but in everything by prayer and
supplication with thanksgiving let your requests be made
known to God. And the peace of God, which surpasses all
understanding, will guard your hearts and your minds in
Christ Jesus. And the God of peace will be with you.

Philippians 4:6-7,9

THE SOUL is immediately at one with God, when it is truly at
peace in itself.

Julian of Norwich

Give us perfect peace, Lord,
so that we may delight in serving you,
all the days of our life,
and at last, with our Lady's help,
come safely to your presence.

Midday Prayer

Lord, give peace to our troubled world; and give to your
children security of mind and freedom from anxiety.

Bidding Prayer

JOY

AS A DEER LONGS for flowing streams,
so my soul longs for you, O God.   *Psalm 42:1*

JESUS SAID:
  "So you have pain now;
  but I will see you again,
  and your hearts will rejoice,
  and no one will take your joy from you."

John 16:22

REJOICE ALWAYS,
pray without ceasing,
give thanks in all circumstances;
for this is the will of God in Christ Jesus for you.

1 Thessalonians 5:16-18

THEN JESUS LOOKED UP AT HIS DISCIPLES and said:
  "Blessed are you who are poor,
  for yours is the kingdom of God.
  Blessed are you who are hungry now,
  for you will be filled.
  Blessed are you who weep now,
  for you will laugh."

Luke 6:20-21

REJOICE IN THE LORD always, again I will say rejoice.

Philippians 4:4

THEREFORE MY HEART IS GLAD, and my soul rejoices;
my body also rests secure.
You show me the path of life.
In your presence there is fullness of joy;
in your right hand are pleasures forevermore.

Psalm 16:9,11

IF YOU abide in love
you will abide in God
and not wander any more in darkness.

Then live in joyfulness and hope
unanxious, without any trace of fear,
at peace with yourself and the world,
in ceaseless reverence and thanks.
Because God's love for you endures for ever.

Rule for a New Brother

Lord God,
you are the source of all that is good,
of all that brings joy.
Help us to rejoice always in you
and to share our joy with others.

The Prayer of the Church

HE will never have full joy in us until we have full joy in him,
truly seeing his lovely blessed face.

Julian of Norwich

LAW

'HEAVEN AND EARTH WILL PASS AWAY but my words will not pass away,' says the Lord.

Matthew 24.35

> LET YOUR MERCY COME TO ME, that I may live;
> for your law is my delight.
>
> *Psalm 119:77*

THEREFORE DEVOTE YOURSELVES completely to the LORD our God, walking in his statutes and keeping his commandments.

1 Kings 8:61

> THE WISE will not hate the law,
> but the one who is hypocritical about it
> is like a boat in a storm.
>
> *Sirach (Ecclesiasticus) 33:2*

OWE NO ONE ANYTHING, except to love one another; for the one who loves another has fulfilled the law. The commandments are summed up in this word, "Love your neighbour as yourself." Love does no wrong to a neighbour; therefore, love is the fulfilling of the law.

from Romans 13:8-10

> Help us to keep your commandments, so that through your Holy Spirit we may dwell in you, and you in us.
>
> *Bidding Prayer*

> Shed your clear light on our hearts, Lord,
> that walking continually in the way of your commandments,
> we may never be deceived or misled.
>
> *Morning Prayer*

THIS IS THE COVENANT that I will make with the house of Israel after those days, says the LORD: I will put my law within them, and I will write it on their hearts; and I will be their God, and they shall be my people.

from Jeremiah 31:33

Love and do what you will.

St Augustine

SO YOU ALSO, when you have done all that you were ordered to do, say, "We are worthless slaves; we have done only what we ought to have done!"

Luke 17:10

UNITY

FINALLY, BROTHERS AND SISTERS, listen to my appeal. Agree with one another, live in peace; and the God of love and peace will be with you. Greet one another with a holy kiss. All the saints greet you. The grace of the Lord Jesus Christ, the love of God, and the communion of the Holy Spirit be with all of you.

from 2 Corinthians 13:11-13

LET THE PEACE OF CHRIST rule in your hearts, to which indeed you were called in the one body. And be thankful.

Colossians 3:15

MAY THE GOD OF STEADFASTNESS and encouragement grant you to live in harmony with one another, in accordance with Christ Jesus, so that together you may with one voice glorify the God and Father of our Lord Jesus Christ.

Romans 15:5-6

I THEREFORE, THE PRISONER IN THE LORD, beg you to lead a life worthy of the calling to which you have been called, with all humility and gentleness, with patience, bearing with one another in love, making every effort to maintain the unity of the Spirit in the bond of peace. There is one body and one Spirit, just as you were called to the one hope of your calling, one Lord, one faith, one baptism, one God and Father of all, who is above all and through all and in all.

Ephesians 4:1-6

EACH OF US WAS GIVEN GRACE according to the measure of Christ's gift. The gifts he gave were that some would be apostles, some prophets, some evangelists, some pastors and teachers, to equip the saints for the work of ministry, for building up the body of Christ, until all of us come to the unity of the faith and of the knowledge of the Son of God, to maturity, to the measure of the full stature of Christ.

Ephesians 4:9,11-13

 Let us pray that everyone
of every race and nation,
may acknowledge the one God as Father,
and in the bond of our common family,
seek his kingdom,
which is peace and joy in the Holy Spirit.

Bidding Prayer, Confirmation

Jesus Christ, the Life

GOD CREATED HUMANKIND in his image,
in the image of God he created them;
male and female he created them.   *Genesis 1:27*

JESUS SAID:
  I came that they may have life,
  and have it abundantly.   *John 10:10*

JESUS died so that we could share God's life. To find this
fullness of life we must die to self, be converted, be patient in
our sufferings and uncertainties, be willing to grow in hope and
love. As we become more aware of God's presence in our lives,
and of the world he has made, so we are ready to adore, to
praise and to thank him. By sharing the life of Christ in his
Church we discover something of the freedom of the sons and
daughters of God.

DEATH

Remember our brothers and sisters
who have gone to their rest
in the hope of rising again;
bring them and all the departed
into the light of your presence.

Eucharistic Prayer

DEATH WAS NEVER OF GOD'S FASHIONING; not for his pleasure
does life cease to be; what meant his creation, but that all
created things should have being? No breed has he created on
earth but for its thriving; none carries in itself the seeds of its
own destruction. Think not that mortality bears sway on earth;
no end or term is fixed to a life well lived.

Wisdom 1:13-15 (Knox)

MY SOUL THIRSTS FOR GOD,
for the living God.
When shall I come and behold
the face of God?

Psalm 42:2

We pray for those who have died,
    and are on their way to you, Lord.
Give them fullness of life and happiness.

We pray for those who are dying, Lord,
    and who are afraid.
Give them strength to go on their last journey in peace.

We pray, Lord, for those who have been wounded
    by the death of one they love.
Help them find the new life that comes through death.

We pray for those who are worried and anxious
    about many things.
Help them, Lord, find peace in dying to themselves.

We pray for those who are depressed and in despair.
Show them, Lord,
    that by dying to self there is a birth of hope.

Bidding Prayers

Lord, Lord, do you hear me?
Lord, show me my door,
take me by the hand.
Open the door,
show me the way,
the path leading to joy, to light.   *Michel Quoist*

CHRIST is the morning star
who, when the darkness of this world is past,
brings to his saints the promise of the light of life
and opens everlasting day.

St Bede

CHRIST when he died
Deceived the cross;
And on death's side
Threw all the loss.
The captive world awaked and found
The prisoner loose, the jailer bound.

Richard Crashaw

LET the absolving words be said over me, and the holy oil
sign and seal me, and thy own body be my food and thy
blood my sprinkling. And let my mother Mary breathe on me
and my angel whisper peace to me, and my saints smile on me,
… that in them all and through them all I may receive the gift
of perseverance, and die, as I desire to live, in thy faith, in thy
Church, in thy service, and in thy love.

Cardinal Newman

Lord God,
you have prepared for those who love you
what no eye has seen, no ear has heard.
Fill our hearts with your love,
so that loving you above all and in all,
we may attain your promises
which the heart of man has not conceived.

Sunday Prayer

IF WE HAVE DIED with him, we will also live with him;
if we endure, we will also reign with him;
if we deny him, he will also deny us;
if we are faithless, he remains faithful –
for he cannot deny himself.

2 Timothy 2:11-13

Day is done, but love unfailing
dwells ever here;
shadows fall, but hope prevailing
calms every fear.
Loving Father, none forsaking,
take our hearts, of love's own making,
watch our sleeping, guard our waking,
be always near!

Dark descends, but light unending
shines through our night;
you are with us, ever lending
new strength to sight;
one in love, your truth confessing,
one in hope of heaven's blessing,
may we see, in love's possessing,
love's endless light!

James Quinn

THE THRONE OF GOD and of the Lamb will be in the city, and his servants will worship him; they will see his face, and his name will be on their foreheads. And there will be no more night; they need no light of lamp or sun, for the Lord God will be their light, and they will reign forever and ever.

Revelation 22:3-5

FATHER, into your hands I commend my spirit.

Luke 23:46

JESUS SAID,
"I am the resurrection and the life.
Those who believe in me,
even though they die, will live,
and everyone who lives and believes in me
will never die."

John 11:25-26

VERY TRULY, I TELL YOU,
unless a grain of wheat falls into the earth and dies,
it remains just a single grain;
but if it dies, it bears much fruit.
Those who love their life lose it,
and those who hate their life in this world
will keep it for eternal life.

John 12:24-25

VERY TRULY, I TELL YOU,
whoever keeps my word
will never see death.

John 8:51

THOSE WHO FIND THEIR LIFE WILL LOSE IT,
and those who lose their life for my sake will find it.

Matthew 10:39

COME, Lord Jesus!

Revelation 22:20

CONVERSION

BEAR FRUIT worthy of repentance.

Matthew 3:8

 Give me, good Lord, a full faith and a fervent charity, a love of you, good Lord, incomparable above the love of myself; and that I love nothing to your displeasure but everything in an order to you. Take from me, good Lord, this lukewarm fashion, or rather key-cold manner of meditation and this dullness in praying to you. And give me warmth, delight and life in thinking about you. And give me your grace to long for your holy Sacraments and specially to rejoice in the presence of your blessed Body, sweet Saviour Christ, in the Holy Sacrament of the Altar, and duly to thank you for your gracious coming.

St Thomas More

FOR THE SON OF MAN came to seek out and to save the lost.

Luke 19:10

FOR JUST AS YOU WERE DISPOSED to go astray from God, return with tenfold zeal to seek him.

Baruch 4:28-29

 Soul of Christ, make me holy.
Body of Christ, save me.
Blood of Christ, fulfil me.
Water from the side of Christ, cleanse me.
Passion of Christ, fortify me.
O Good Jesus, hear me.
Within your wounds Lord, lose me.
Never let me leave you.
From all evil protect me.

Through death's door, beckon me.
And call me to you,
so may I join the saints in praising you,
Always and for ever. Amen.

The Anima Christi (Soul of Christ)

I WILL MAKE AN EVERLASTING COVENANT with them, never to draw back from doing good to them; and I will put the fear of me in their hearts, so that they may not turn from me.

Jeremiah 32:40

TRULY I TELL YOU, unless you change and become like children, you will never enter the kingdom of heaven.

Matthew 18:3

YOU WERE TAUGHT to put away your former way of life, your old self, and to be renewed in the spirit of your minds, and to clothe yourselves with the new self, created according to the likeness of God in true righteousness and holiness.

from Ephesians 4:22-24

 O God, give me the sincerity
to accept the things I cannot change,
the courage to change the things I can,
and the wisdom to know the difference.

Rheinhold Niebuhr

PATIENCE

WE ALSO BOAST IN OUR SUFFERINGS, knowing that suffering produces endurance, and endurance produces character, and character produces hope, and hope does not disappoint us, because God's love has been poured into our hearts through the Holy Spirit that has been given to us.

Romans 5:3-5

WITH THE LORD ONE DAY IS LIKE A THOUSAND YEARS, and a thousand years are like one day. The Lord is not slow about his promise, as some think of slowness, but is patient with you, not wanting any to perish, but all to come to repentance.

2 Peter 3:8-9

LOVE IS PATIENT, love is kind.

1 Corinthians 13:4

REMEMBER, O most loving Virgin Mary, that it is a thing unheard of, that anyone ever had recourse to your protection, implored your help, or sought your intercession, and was left forsaken. Filled therefore with confidence in your goodness I fly to you, O Mother, Virgin of virgins. To you I come, before you I stand, a sorrowful sinner. Despise not my poor words, O Mother of the Word of God, but graciously hear and grant my prayer.

St Bernard

Lord, give me patience in tribulation. Let the memory of your Passion, and of those bitter pains you suffered for me, strengthen my patience and support me in this tribulation and adversity.

St John Forrest

 Give patient tolerance, Lord, to all who are no longer young. Open the hearts of the young to accept from them understanding and love.

Bidding Prayer

Never disappoint the trust
another puts in you.
Be warm and merciful
and let none go from you empty-handed.
The least you can offer
is your time and patience,
your affection and your prayer.

Rule for a New Brother

O Lord my God, as you led your people through the desert, so lead me now through the desert of my failures to your kingdom. Light my way; show me your will; give me your Spirit of truth, so that I may know, love and serve you more faithfully.

SUFFERING

A LL shall be well, and all shall be well, and all manner of things shall be well.

Julian of Norwich

Lord, in answer to our prayer
give us patience in suffering hardships
after the example of your only-begotten Son,
who lives and reigns for ever and ever. Amen

Midday Prayer

Lord, teach us to see you present in all people. Help us to recognise you most of all in those who suffer.

Bidding Prayer

"MY FATHER, if it is possible, let this cup pass from me; yet not what I want but what you want. My Father, if this cannot pass unless I drink it, your will be done."

Matthew 26:39,42

THE SPIRIT INDEED IS WILLING, but the flesh is weak.

Matthew 26:41

I CONSIDER that the sufferings of this present time are not worth comparing with the glory about to be revealed to us. For the creation waits with eager longing for the revealing of the children of God; and not only the creation, but we ourselves, who have the first fruits of the Spirit, groan inwardly while we wait for adoption, the redemption of our bodies… We wait for it with patience.

from Romans 8:18-25

I HAVE BEEN CRUCIFIED WITH CHRIST; and it is no longer I who
live, but it is Christ who lives in me.

Galatians 2:19-20

MY GOD, MY GOD, why have you forsaken me?
Do not be far from me,
    for trouble is near and there is no one to help.

O LORD, do not be far away!
O my help, come quickly to my aid!

Psalm 22:1,11,19

 Lord, be with those who are persecuted for their
faith, and those cut off from the support of the
Church; good Shepherd, in their pain and
desolation may they know your tender care.

Bidding Prayer

GROWTH

FOR THIS REASON, since the day we heard it, we have not ceased
praying for you and asking that you may be filled with the
knowledge of God's will in all spiritual wisdom and
understanding, so that you may lead lives worthy of the Lord,
fully pleasing to him, as you bear fruit in every good work and
as you grow in the knowledge of God. May you be made strong
with all the strength that comes from his glorious power, and
may you be prepared to endure everything with patience, while
joyfully giving thanks to the Father, who has enabled you to
share in the inheritance of the saints in the light.

Colossians 1:9-12

LET LOVE BE GENUINE; hate what is evil, hold fast to what is good;
love one another with mutual affection; outdo one another in
showing honour. Do not lag in zeal, be ardent in spirit, serve the
Lord. Rejoice in hope, be patient in suffering, persevere in prayer.

Romans 12:9-12

MY BROTHERS AND SISTERS, whenever you face trials of any kind, consider it nothing but joy, because you know that the testing of your faith produces endurance; and let endurance have its full effect, so that you may be mature and complete, lacking in nothing.

James 1:2-4

The glory of God is Man made fully alive.   *St Irenaeus*

HOW high thou art in the height, how deep in the depth. Thou never leavest us, yet how hard it is to return to thee. Come, Lord, and work. Arouse and incite us. Kindle us and sweep us onward. Be fragrant as flowers, sweet as honey. Teach us to love and to run.

St Augustine

JESUS SAID:
"Very truly, I tell you,
unless you eat the flesh of the Son of Man
and drink his blood,
you have no life in you.
Those who eat my flesh and drink my blood
have eternal life,
and I will raise them up on the last day;
for my flesh is true food and my blood is true drink.
Those who eat my flesh and drink my blood
abide in me, and I in them…
The one who eats this bread will live forever."

from John 6:53-58

 Almighty God and Father, you so loved the world that you sent your Son to show us how to love without limit. Teach me to accept your Spirit of love and truth so that I may learn to live as your friend.

PERSONAL growth is not optional for us … God's will that we must grow sums up our human duty.   *Pope Paul VI*

HOPE

> THE LORD IS MY SHEPHERD,
> I shall not want.
> He makes me lie down in green pastures;
> he leads me beside still waters;
> he restores my soul.
> He leads me in right paths for his name's sake.

Psalm 23:1-3

LET US THEREFORE approach the throne of grace with boldness, so that we may receive mercy and find grace to help in time of need.

Hebrews 4:16

> WHEN I AM AFRAID, I put my trust in you.
> In God, whose word I praise,
> in God I trust; I am not afraid;
> what can flesh do to me?

Psalm 56:4-5

JESUS SAID: "Truly I tell you, today you will be with me in Paradise."

Luke 23:43

WE ARE AFFLICTED IN EVERY WAY, but not crushed; perplexed, but not driven to despair; persecuted, but not forsaken; struck down, but not destroyed; always carrying in the body the death of Jesus, so that the life of Jesus may also be made visible in our bodies.

2 Corinthians 4:8-10

O God, to whom all hearts are open, all desires
known, and from whom no secrets are hidden,
cleanse the thoughts of our hearts by the in
pouring of your Holy Spirit, that every thought
and word of ours may begin from you, and in you
be perfectly completed, through Christ our Lord.
Amen.

A Confirmation Prayer

REDEEM ME, LORD, and be gracious to me.

Psalm 25(26):11

BLESSED ARE THOSE WHO TRUST IN THE LORD,
whose trust is the LORD.
They shall be like a tree planted by water,
sending out its roots by the stream.
It shall not fear when heat comes,
and its leaves shall stay green;
in the year of drought it is not anxious,
and it does not cease to bear fruit.

Jeremiah 17:7-8

O TASTE AND SEE that the LORD is good;
happy are those who take refuge in him.

Psalm 34:8

O God, the creator and redeemer of all the
faithful, grant to the souls of your servants
departed the remission of all their sins, that
through our prayers they may obtain that pardon
which they have always desired.

Prayer for the Dead

LOVE

Lord God,
you love us as a father loves his children.
Help us to respond to your gift
and learn to love without limit,
as did your Son,
Jesus Christ, our Lord.

LOVE IS PATIENT; LOVE IS KIND; love is not envious or boastful
or arrogant or rude. It does not insist on its own way; it is not
irritable or resentful; it does not rejoice in wrongdoing, but
rejoices in the truth. It bears all things, believes all things,
hopes all things, endures all things. Love never ends… And
now faith, hope, and love abide, these three; and the greatest of
these is love.

1 Corinthians 13:4-13

God of your goodness give me yourself, for you
are enough for me.

Julian of Norwich

MAY THE LORD MAKE YOU INCREASE AND ABOUND IN LOVE for
one another and for all, just as we abound in love for you. And
may he so strengthen your hearts in holiness that you may be
blameless before our God and Father at the coming of our Lord
Jesus with all his saints.

1 Thessalonians 3:12-13

GOD IS LOVE,
and those who abide in love abide in God,
and God abides in them.

1 John 4:16

The perfect lover longeth for to be
In presence of his love both night and day
And if it haply so befall that he may not be as he would,
He will yet as he may ever be with his love.   *St Thomas More*

 Jesus, grant us grace truly to love you for your
great goodness and the generous gifts we have
received, and hope always to receive from you.

Jesus, Jesus, Jesus}
Jesus, Jesus, Jesus} **Grant us grace to love you!**
Jesus, Jesus, Jesus}

Let the thought of your goodness and patience overcome
our sinful inclinations. (Jesus, Jesus, Jesus...)

Let the consideration of the times you have come into our
lives to help and save us, make us ashamed of our
ingratitude. (Jesus, Jesus, Jesus...)

To think that you ask nothing of us in return, except that
we should love you, and you ask that only because you are
so good! (Jesus, Jesus, Jesus...)

Dear Lord, our whole life shall be nothing but a desire for
you, and to show our love we shall keep your
commandments faithfully. (Jesus, Jesus, Jesus...)

Have mercy on all sinners, Jesus, we beg you; turn their
vices into virtues, convert their hearts to love of you and
your commandments and bring them to bliss in
everlasting glory. (Jesus, Jesus, Jesus...)

Have mercy also on the souls in purgatory, for your bitter
Passion, we beg you, and for your glorious name, Jesus.
(Our Father ... Hail Mary ...)

from The Jesus Psalter

BELOVED, let us love one another,
because love is from God;
everyone who loves is born of God and knows God…
No one has ever seen God;
if we love one another, God lives in us,
and his love is perfected in us…
God is love,
and those who abide in love abide in God,
and God abides in them.

1 John 4:7-16

FOR GOD SO LOVED THE WORLD
that he gave his only Son,
so that everyone who believes in him
may not perish
but may have eternal life.

John 3:16

Where true love is dwelling, God is dwelling there;
Love's own loving presence love does ever share.

Love of Christ has made us out of many one;
In our midst is dwelling God's eternal Son.

Give him joyful welcome, love him and revere;
Cherish one another with a love sincere.

James Quinn

 O heart of love, I put all my trust in thee. For I
fear all things from my own weakness, but I hope
for all things from thy goodness.

St Margaret Mary

THIS IS MY COMMANDMENT,
that you love one another
as I have loved you.

John 15:12

LITTLE CHILDREN, LET US LOVE, not in word or speech,
but in truth and action.

1 John 3:18

FOR I AM CONVINCED that neither death, nor life, nor angels, nor rulers, nor things present, nor things to come, nor powers, nor height, nor depth, nor anything else in all creation, will be able to separate us from the love of God in Christ Jesus our Lord.

Romans 8:38-39

RISE UP, COME TO OUR HELP. Redeem us for the sake of your steadfast love. *Psalm 44:26*

Jesus, grant me the grace to love you.
O blessed Jesu, make me love you entirely.
O blessed Jesu, let me deeply consider your love
    for me.
O blessed Jesu, give me the grace to thank you
    for your gifts.
Sweet Jesu, possess my heart, hold and keep it
    for yourself alone. *St John Fisher*

THE PRESENCE OF GOD

I WALK BEFORE THE LORD
in the land of the living. *Psalm 116:9*

BE STILL, and know that I am God! *Psalm 46:10*

FOR WHERE TWO OR THREE ARE GATHERED in my name, I am there among them. *Matthew 18:20*

THOSE WHO LOVE ME will keep my word,
and my Father will love them,
and we will come to them
and make our home with them. *John 14:23*

Alone with none but thee, my God,
I journey on my way;
What need I fear, when thou art near,
O King of night and day?
More safe am I within thy hand
Than if a host did round me stand.

St Columba

WHEN my strength fails me and I cannot even say my prayers, I repeat: "Jesus, here I am; I'm Francis." Joy and consolation come, and I experience Jesus responding: "Francis, here I am; I'm Jesus."

Cardinal Francis Nguyen Van Thuan
for 9 years in solitary confinement in Vietnam

GOD ABIDES in those
who confess that Jesus is the Son of God,
and they abide in God.

1 John 4:15

WE are enfolded in the Father, we are enfolded in the Son, and we are enfolded in the Holy Spirit. And the Father is enfolded in us, and the Son is enfolded in us, and the Holy Spirit is enfolded in us.

Julian of Norwich

Lord, true light and creator of light,
grant that faithfully pondering on all that is holy,
we may ever live in the splendour of your presence.

Morning Prayer

O gracious and holy Father,
give us wisdom to perceive you,
intelligence to understand you,
diligence to seek you,
patience to wait for you,
eye to behold you,
a heart to meditate upon you,
and a life to proclaim you;
through the power of the Spirit
of Jesus Christ our Lord.

St Benedict

God be in my head and in my understanding;
God be in mine eyes, and in my looking;
God be in my mouth, and in my speaking;
God be in my heart, and in my thinking;
God be at mine end, and at my departing.

Book of Hours, 1514

NOW TO HIM WHO BY THE POWER at work within us is able to accomplish abundantly far more than all we can ask or imagine, to him be glory in the church and in Christ Jesus to all generations, forever and ever. Amen.

Ephesians 3:20-21

YOU ARE BEING PROTECTED by the power of God through faith for a salvation ready to be revealed in the last time.

1 Peter 1:5

O God come to my aid,
O Lord make haste to help me!

The Prayer of the Church

CHRIST WAS CRUCIFIED IN WEAKNESS, but lives by the power of God. For we are weak in him, but in dealing with you we will live with him by the power of God.

2 Corinthians 13:4

MY GRACE IS SUFFICIENT FOR YOU, for power is made perfect in weakness.

2 Corinthians 12:9

THE RIGHT HAND OF THE LORD is exalted;
the right hand of the LORD does valiantly.
I shall not die, but I shall live,
and recount the deeds of the LORD.

Psalm 118:16-17

It were my soul's desire
to see the face of God;
it were my soul's desire
to rest in his abode.

Grant, Lord, my soul's desire,
deep waves of cleansing sighs,
grant, Lord, my soul's desire.
from earthly cares to rise.

It were my soul's desire
to imitate my King,
it were my soul's desire
his endless praise to sing.

It were my soul's desire,
when heaven's gate is won,
to find my soul's desire
clear shining like the sun.

This still my soul's desire,
whatever life afford,
to gain my soul's desire,
and see thy face, O Lord.

The Prayer of the Church

CREATION

HOW GREAT ARE YOUR WORKS, O LORD!
Your thoughts are very deep.   *Psalm 92:6*

GOD SAW EVERYTHING THAT HE HAD MADE, and indeed,
it was very good.   *Genesis 1:31*

LONG AGO you laid the foundation of the earth,
and the heavens are the work of your hands.
                                                Psalm 102:25

Blessed are you, Lord, God of all creation.
Through your goodness we have ourselves to offer,
whom you have made and called to be your children.
May we live indeed as the work of your hands.
Blessed be God for ever.   *An Offertory Prayer*

THE HEAVENS ARE TELLING THE GLORY OF GOD;
and the firmament proclaims his handiwork.
Day to day pours forth speech,
and night to night declares knowledge.

There is no speech, nor are there words;
their voice is not heard;
yet their voice goes out through all the earth,
and their words to the end of the world.

In the heavens he has set a tent for the sun,
which comes out like a bridegroom from his wedding
        canopy,
and like a strong man runs its course with joy.

Its rising is from the end of the heavens,
and its circuit to the end of them;
and nothing is hid from its heat.   *Psalm 19:1-6*

O thou, who art the true sun of the world, ever rising, and never going down; who by thy most wholesome appearing and sight dost nourish and gladden all things in heaven and earth; we beseech thee mercifully to shine into our hearts, that the night and darkness of sin, and the mists of error on every side, being driven away by the brightness of thy shining within our hearts, we may all our life walk without stumbling, as in the day time, and being pure and clean from the works of darkness, may abound in all good works which thou hadst prepared for us to walk in. Amen.

Erasmus

FOR LO, THE ONE WHO FORMS THE MOUNTAINS,
creates the wind,
reveals his thoughts to mortals,
makes the morning darkness,
and treads on the heights of the earth—
the LORD, the God of hosts, is his name!

Amos 4:13

PRAISE AND THANKSGIVING

BLESS THE LORD, O MY SOUL,
and all that is within me, bless his holy name.
Bless the LORD, O my soul,
and do not forget all his benefits.   *Psalm 103:1-2*

O GIVE THANKS to the LORD, for he is good;
for his steadfast love endures forever!

Psalm 107:1

LET EVERYTHING THAT BREATHES praise the LORD!
Praise the LORD.

Psalm 150:6

THE LORD GAVE, and the LORD has taken away; blessed
be the name of the LORD.

Job 1:21

 Thanks be to you, my Lord Jesus Christ,
for all the benefits which you have given me,
for all the pains and insults
which you have borne for me.
O most merciful Redeemer, Friend and Brother,
may I know you more clearly,
love you more dearly,
follow you more nearly,
day by day.

St Richard of Chichester

LET THE WORD OF CHRIST DWELL IN YOU RICHLY; teach and
admonish one another in all wisdom; and with gratitude in
your hearts sing psalms, hymns, and spiritual songs to God.
And whatever you do, in word or deed, do everything in the
name of the Lord Jesus, giving thanks to God the Father
through him.

Colossians 3:16-17

SO, WHETHER YOU EAT OR DRINK, or whatever you do, do
everything for the glory of God.

1 Corinthians 10:31

The Lord's is the earth and its fullness.
Come let us adore him!   *Antiphon*

O GIVE THANKS to the LORD, for he is good;
his steadfast love endures forever!

Psalm 118:1

YOU ARE WORTHY, our Lord and God, to receive glory and
honour and power, for you created all things, and by your will
they existed and were created.

Revelation 4:11

O THE DEPTH OF THE RICHES and wisdom and knowledge of God! How unsearchable are his judgments and how inscrutable his ways! For who has known the mind of the Lord? Or who has been his counsellor? Or who has given a gift to him, to receive a gift in return? For from him and through him and to him are all things. To him be the glory forever. Amen.

Romans 11:33-36

THE CHURCH

JESUS PUT BEFORE THEM ANOTHER PARABLE:
"The kingdom of heaven is like a mustard seed that someone took and sowed in his field; it is the smallest of all the seeds, but when it has grown it is the greatest of shrubs and becomes a tree, so that the birds of the air come and make nests in its branches."
He told them another parable:
"The kingdom of heaven is like yeast that a woman took and mixed in with three measures of flour until all of it was leavened.
"And again: The kingdom of heaven is like treasure hidden in a field, which someone found and hid; then in his joy he goes and sells all that he has and buys that field.
"Again, the kingdom of heaven is like a merchant in search of fine pearls; on finding one pearl of great value, he went and sold all that he had and bought it.
"Again, the kingdom of heaven is like a net that was thrown into the sea and caught fish of every kind; when it was full, they drew it ashore, sat down, and put the good into baskets but threw out the bad."

from Matthew 13:31-49

JESUS SAID: "I tell you, you are Peter, and on this rock I will build my church, and the gates of Hades will not prevail against it. I will give you the keys of the kingdom of heaven, and whatever you bind on earth will be bound in heaven, and whatever you loose on earth will be loosed in heaven."

Matthew 16:18-19

THEY DEVOTED THEMSELVES to the apostles' teaching and fellowship, to the breaking of bread and the prayers.

Awe came upon everyone, because many wonders and signs were being done by the apostles. All who believed were together and had all things in common; they would sell their possessions and goods and distribute the proceeds to all, as any had need. Day by day, as they spent much time together in the temple, they broke bread at home and ate their food with glad and generous hearts, praising God and having the goodwill of all the people. And day by day the Lord added to their number those who were being saved.

Acts 2:42-47

YOU SHALL BE MY PEOPLE, and I will be your God.

Ezekiel 36:28

YOU ARE A CHOSEN RACE, a royal priesthood, a holy nation, God's own people, in order that you may proclaim the mighty acts of him who called you out of darkness into his marvellous light. Once you were not a people, but now you are God's people

1 Peter 2:9-10

 May your Church, Lord, be a light to the nations, the sign and source of your power to unite all people. May she lead mankind to the mystery of your love.

Bidding Prayer.

FREEDOM

F OR we know that the law is spiritual; but I am of the flesh, sold into slavery under sin. I do not understand my own actions. For I do not do what I want, but I do the very thing I hate. Now if I do what I do not want, I agree that the law is good. But in fact it is no longer I that do it, but sin that dwells within me. For I know that nothing good dwells within me, that is, in my flesh. I can will what is right, but I cannot do it. For I do not do the good I want, but the evil I do not want is what I do. Now if I do what I do not want, it is no longer I that do it, but sin that dwells within me. So I find it to be a law that when I want to do what is good, evil lies close at hand. For I delight in the law of God in my inmost self, but I see in my members another law at war with the law of my mind, making me captive to the law of sin that dwells in my members. Wretched man that I am! Who will rescue me from this body of death? Thanks be to God through Jesus Christ our Lord! So then, with my mind I am a slave to the law of God, but with my flesh I am a slave to the law of sin.

Romans 7:14-25

BUT THOSE WHO LOOK INTO THE PERFECT LAW, the law of liberty, and persevere, being not hearers who forget but doers who act—they will be blessed in their doing.

James 1:25

You, Lord, are the source of our freedom. Bring those in captivity of mind or body to the freedom of the children of God.

Bidding Prayer

SO IF THE SON MAKES YOU FREE, you will be free indeed.

John 8:36

FOR WHOEVER WAS CALLED in the Lord as a slave is a freed person belonging to the Lord, just as whoever was free when called is a slave of Christ.

1 Corinthians 7:22

FOR IF WE HAVE BEEN UNITED with him in a death like his, we will certainly be united with him in a resurrection like his. We know that our old self was crucified with him so that the body of sin might be destroyed, and we might no longer be enslaved to sin. For whoever has died is freed from sin.

Romans 6:5-7

IF YOU CONTINUE IN MY WORD,
you are truly my disciples;
and you will know the truth,
and the truth will make you free.

John 8:31-32

AS MANY OF YOU AS WERE BAPTIZED into Christ have clothed yourselves with Christ. There is no longer Jew or Greek, there is no longer slave or free, there is no longer male and female; for all of you are one in Christ Jesus.

Galatians 3:27-28

AS SERVANTS OF GOD, live as free people, yet do not use your freedom as a pretext for evil. Honour everyone. Love the family of believers. Fear God.

1 Peter 2:16-17

FOR ALL WHO ARE LED BY THE SPIRIT OF GOD are children of God. For you did not receive a spirit of slavery to fall back into fear, but you have received a spirit of adoption. When we cry, "Abba! Father!" it is that very Spirit bearing witness with our spirit that we are children of God, and if children, then heirs, heirs of God and joint heirs with Christ—if, in fact, we suffer with him so that we may also be glorified with him.

Romans 8:14-17

THE SPIRIT OF THE LORD GOD is upon me,
because the LORD has anointed me;
he has sent me to bring good news to the oppressed,
  to bind up the broken hearted,
to proclaim liberty to the captives,
and release to the prisoners;
to proclaim the year of the LORD'S favour.

Isaiah 61:1-2

Jubilee

THE Great Jubilee is a time of Blessing, of Reconciliation, of Sharing, of Thanksgiving, of Renewal. It is the Lord's year of favour promised by Jesus.

"THE SPIRIT OF THE LORD is upon me, because he has anointed me to bring good news to the poor. He has sent me to proclaim release to the captives and recovery of sight to the blind, to let the oppressed go free, to proclaim the year of the Lord's favour." And he rolled up the scroll, gave it back to the attendant, and sat down. The eyes of all in the synagogue were fixed on him. Then he began to say to them, "Today this scripture has been fulfilled in your hearing." All spoke well of him and were amazed at the gracious words that came from his mouth.

from Luke 4:18-22

SEE, he is the Lord our God. See him, the mediator between God and humanity, a human being and our saviour. Son of the Father; his mother bore him; born thus from the flesh of his mother, he glorified the Father.

St Augustine

Christ today, Christ yesterday,
Christ who was and is to come.
You are God and you are love
And you call us here today

from Hymn for the celebration of the Great Jubilee

Lord, you called out
to all those overburdened,
to all the weary,
to all those weighed down with cares,
to seek rest in you.
At this time of Jubilee grace we pray
for all those who cry out for help,
for all victims of persecution,
for all those crushed by injustice,
for all those suffering hunger or poverty,
for all those weary in life.
May this time of blessing
bring rest to tired bodies,
new life to weary spirits,
help to burdened souls.
May this time of renewal
change unbelieving minds to faith,
melt cold hearts to love,
inspire leaders to govern with justice,
so that in the new millennium our world
may become a better place.
Amen.

Columban Fathers

Let there be…
Respect for the earth
Peace for its people
Love in our lives
Delight in the good
Forgiveness for past wrongs
And from now on a new start

Millennium Prayer: New Start 2000

BLESSING

Heavenly Father.
you have shown your love for us
by giving us Jesus to be our way to you.
Guide us all on our journey.
Bless us with peace and joy
and bring us to our home with you.

from A Book of Blessings

WHEN THEY HAD FINISHED EVERYTHING required by the law of
the Lord, they returned to Galilee, to their own town of
Nazareth. The child grew and became strong, filled with
wisdom; and the favour of God was upon him. Then he went
down with them and came to Nazareth, and was obedient to
them. His mother treasured all these things in her heart. And
Jesus increased in wisdom and in years, and in divine and
human favour.

Luke 2:39-40, 51-52

I AM young and I possess many buried qualities; I am young
and strong and am living a great adventure; I am still in the
midst of it and can't grumble the whole day long. I have been
given a lot, a happy nature, a great deal of cheerfulness and

strength. Every day I feel that I am developing inwardly, that the liberation is drawing nearer and how beautiful nature is, how good the people are about me, how interesting this adventure is! Why, then, should I be in despair?

The Diary of Anne Frank

 There is in me…
an awakening, a strength,
a joy, a purposefulness,
a future, a life that knows no end.
God be praised for what I am,
and what I may become!   *DK*

I T IS not God's way that great blessings should descend without the sacrifice first of great sufferings.

John Henry Newman

 May the Lord bless you and protect you.
May he let his face shine upon you and be
gracious to you.
May he look upon you with kindness and give
you his peace.

A traditional blessing

RECONCILIATION

JESUS TOLD THIS PARABLE.
"There was a man who had two sons. The younger of them said to his father, 'Father, give me the share of the property that will belong to me.' So he divided his property between them. A few days later the younger son gathered all he had and travelled to a distant country, and there he squandered his property in dissolute living. But when he came to himself he set off and went to his father. But while he was still far off, his father saw

him and was filled with compassion; he ran and put his arms around him and kissed him. Then the son said to him, 'Father, I have sinned against heaven and before you; I am no longer worthy to be called your son.' But the father said to his slaves, 'Quickly, bring out a robe—the best one—and put it on him; put a ring on his finger and sandals on his feet. And get the fatted calf and kill it, and let us eat and celebrate; for this son of mine was dead and is alive again; he was lost and is found!' And they began to celebrate."

from Luke 5:11-24

IT must be recalled that [sacramental] reconciliation with God leads, as it were, to other reconciliations, which repair the other breaches caused by sin. The forgiven penitent is reconciled with himself in his inmost being, where he regains his innermost truth. He is reconciled with his brethren whom he has in some way offended and wounded. He is reconciled with the Church. He is reconciled with all creation.

Pope John Paul II

ALOVE of reconciliation is not weakness or cowardice. It demands courage, nobility, generosity, sometimes heroism, an overcoming of oneself rather than of one's adversary. At times it may even seem like dishonour, but it never offends against true justice or denies the rights of the poor. In reality, it is the patient, wise art of peace, of loving, of living with one's fellows, after the example of Christ, with a strength of heart and mind modelled on his.

Pope Paul VI

SO WHEN YOU ARE OFFERING YOUR GIFT at the altar, if you remember that your brother or sister has something against you, leave your gift there before the altar and go; first be reconciled to your brother or sister, and then come and offer your gift.

Matthew 5:23-24

SHARING

JESUS CAME TO SIMON PETER, who said to him, "Lord, are you going to wash my feet?" He answered, "You do not know now what I am doing, but later you will understand." Peter said to him, "You will never wash my feet." Jesus answered, "Unless I wash you, you have no share with me." Simon Peter said to him, "Lord, not my feet only but also my hands and my head!"

John 13:6-9

GOD'S love is "everlasting": "For the mountains may depart and the hills be removed, but my steadfast love shall not depart from you." Through Jeremiah, God declares to his people, "I have loved you with an everlasting love; therefore I have continued my faithfulness to you." But St. John goes even further when he affirms that "God is love": God's very being is love. By sending his only Son and the Spirit of Love in the fullness of time, God has revealed his innermost secret: God himself is an eternal exchange of love, Father, Son and Holy Spirit, and he has destined us to share in that exchange.

Catechism of the Catholic Church, 220

JESUS SAID: "They who have my commandments and keep them are those who love me; and those who love me will be loved by my Father, and I will love them and reveal myself to them. Those who love me will keep my word, and my Father will love them, and we will come to them and make our home with them."

John 14:21, 23

The community is the place where you daily share riches and poverty, energy and weakness,

> joy and sorrow,
> success and failure
> your hope and your doubt.
> In this kind of community can grow
> something of Christ's bond with his Father:
> 'All that I have is yours,
> all that you have is mine.'
>
> *Rule for a New Brother*

GIVE, AND IT WILL BE GIVEN TO YOU. A good measure, pressed down, shaken together, running over, will be put into your lap; for the measure you give will be the measure you get back.

Luke 6:38

THANKSGIVING

JOB SAID, "Naked I came from my mother's womb, and naked shall I return there; the LORD gave, and the LORD has taken away; blessed be the name of the LORD."

Job 1:21

> MAY THE NAME OF THE LORD endure forever,
> his fame continue as long as the sun.
> May all nations be blessed in him;
> may they pronounce him happy.
> Blessed be the LORD, the God of Israel,
> who alone does wondrous things.
> Blessed be his glorious name forever;
> may his glory fill the whole earth. Amen and Amen.
>
> *Psalm 72:17-19*

DO NOT WORRY ABOUT ANYTHING, but in everything by prayer and supplication with thanksgiving let your requests be made known to God.

Philippians 4:6

GIVE THANKS IN ALL CIRCUMSTANCES; for this is the will of God in Christ Jesus for you.   *1 Thessalonians 5:18*

> Blessed are you, Lord, God of all creation.
> Through your goodness we have this bread to offer,
> which earth has given and human hands have made.
> It will become for us the bread of life.
>   Blessed be God for ever!
> Blessed are you, Lord, God of all creation.
> Through your goodness we have this wine to offer,
> fruit of the vine, and work of human hands.
> It will become our spiritual drink.
>   Blessed be God for ever!

from the Liturgy of the Eucharist

RENEWAL

AND I SAW THE HOLY CITY, the new Jerusalem, coming down out of heaven from God, prepared as a bride adorned for her husband. And I heard a loud voice from the throne saying, "See, the home of God is among mortals. He will dwell with them as their God; they will be his peoples, and God himself will be with them; he will wipe every tear from their eyes. Death will be no more; mourning and crying and pain will be no more, for the first things have passed away." And the one who was seated on the throne said, "See, I am making all things new." Also he said, "Write this, for these words are trustworthy and true."

Revelation 21:2-5

IT IS therefore necessary to inspire in all the faithful a true longing for holiness, a deep desire for conversion and personal renewal in a context of ever more intense prayer and of solidarity with one's neighbour, especially the most needy.

Pope John Paul II

FOR WE OURSELVES WERE ONCE FOOLISH, disobedient, led astray, slaves to various passions and pleasures, passing our days in malice and envy, despicable, hating one another. But when the goodness and loving kindness of God our Saviour appeared, he saved us, not because of any works of righteousness that we had done, but according to his mercy, through the water of rebirth and renewal by the Holy Spirit. This Spirit he poured out on us richly through Jesus Christ our Saviour, so that, having been justified by his grace, we might become heirs according to the hope of eternal life.

Titus 3:3-6

Holy Spirit, God of Love,
Come, and let fall from above,
    Ray of your light.

Father, come to those in need,
Come rewarding every deed,
    Light of our hearts.

You the one who best consoles,
You most welcome guest of souls,
    Refuge and rest.

Respite in the toil of life,
Subduer of the passions' strife,
    Comfort in grief.

Light that blessedness imparts,
Fill the inmost core of hearts,
    Faithful and true.

In your absence, all in pain,
Man's endeavour all in vain,
    Harmful all things.

What is soiled wash again,
What is arid bless with rain,
    What wounded, heal.

Warm again the love grown cold,
What unyielding, shape and mould,
   What wayward, rule.

Give to faithful hearts confessing,
Gifts beyond all else possessing,
   Seven-fold worth.

Crown the strivings of the soul,
Give, when we have reached the goal,
   Joy evermore.

Veni Sancte Spiritus, trans. Brian Moore

JOURNEY'S END

THE end of our pilgrim journey is our meeting with the Risen Christ. "Christ is risen! He is risen indeed!" we proclaim.

We say: "I believe in the resurrection of the dead and the life everlasting". Then we continue: "This is our faith, this is the faith of the Church, and we are proud to profess it in Christ Jesus our Lord."

Baptismal Promises

O Death, where is thy sting? O Hell, where is thy victory? Christ is risen and the demons have fallen. Christ is risen and the angels rejoice. Christ is risen and life exults. Christ is risen and there is none dead in the tomb. For Christ is raised from the dead, and become the first-fruits of them that slept. To him be glory and dominion for ever and ever. Amen.

St John Chrysostom

A Meditation on
the Mysteries of
the Rosary

THE JOYFUL MYSTERIES

The Annunciation

IN the sixth month the angel Gabriel was sent by God to a town in Galilee called Nazareth, to a virgin engaged to a man whose name was Joseph, of the house of David. The virgin's name was Mary. And he came to her and said, "Greetings, favoured one! The Lord is with you. You will conceive in your womb and bear a son, and you will name him Jesus. He will be great, and will be called the Son of the Most High." Mary said to the angel, "How can this be, since I am a virgin?" The angel said to her, "The Holy Spirit will come upon you, and the power of the Most High will overshadow you; therefore the child to be born will be holy; he will be called Son of God." Then Mary said, "Here am I, the servant of the Lord; let it be with me according to your word." Then the angel departed from her.

from Luke 1:26-38

What a frightening invitation, to become mother of such a
    child…
a child of infinite promise.
One can imagine the sudden clutch of fear…
    the puzzlement…
    the anxiety about the future.
Surely he doesn't mean me?
    But in a moment the fears are stilled,
    and all is seen to be possible.
    "Be it done to me according to your word."

What is my annunciation? When has God sent his angel to me
to announce his Good News? And how have I reacted to the
promises he has made to me?

God's messengers do come to me;
    they tell me that I'm highly favoured…
    much graced and blessed…
    with much fruit to bear…
    and they tell me, too, that the Lord is with me.

But often I do not recognise God's friends,
    because their words are so demanding,
    and I am afraid.

Everyone is blessed by God…
    he has no favourites.
God is with all his people…
    he cannot forget any one of them.
All are chosen people…
    each one unique…
    every person special.
"Do not be afraid," he says to me, "for I have redeemed you;
I have called you by your name and you are mine."

I have been called by God to do him some definite service…
I have a vocation to become what he calls me to be.
If I am ever to answer this call
    I must learn to say,
    "Yes… Let it be done… Let it be done…
    Let it be done to me according to your word."

I must let go –
    of fear…
    of a sense of inadequacy…
    of selfishness and pride…
    of wanting to have everything planned before I make
    a move.
Then I may learn to trust in God; who is Father, Friend,
Tremendous Lover; who knows what I can do, and to whom
nothing is impossible.

        Speak, Lord, your servant hears!

The Visitation

IN those days Mary set out and went with haste to a Judean
town in the hill country, where she entered the house of
Zechariah and greeted Elizabeth. When Elizabeth heard Mary's
greeting, the child leaped in her womb. And Elizabeth was filled
with the Holy Spirit and exclaimed with a loud cry, "Blessed are
you among women, and blessed is the fruit of your womb. And
why has this happened to me, that the mother of my Lord comes
to me? For as soon as I heard the sound of your greeting, the
child in my womb leaped for joy. And blessed is she who
believed that there would be a fulfilment of what was spoken to
her by the Lord." And Mary remained with her about three
months and then returned to her home.

Luke 1:39-45, 56

It is a sign of generosity to be willing to share in another's happiness. Mary's first thought after the angel had left her was to visit her cousin Elizabeth, who "in her old age had herself conceived a son".

There was respect in this visit…
    also thoughtfulness…
    and a certain delicacy.

Elizabeth was an older woman… perhaps she was unsure of the future… she must have welcomed the help and companionship… all Mary could give were her time and herself… gifts that really count.

The generous gift brings a heartfelt response:
    "Blessed is she who believed
    that the promise made her by the Lord
    would be fulfilled."

This is another Beatitude:
I am really blessed if I believe
    in the love of God which enfolds me…
    in the truth of his Word, which speaks to me…
    in the power of his Spirit, which overshadows me.
Then I shall know that "the Almighty has done great things for me", and that I shall live for ever.

First, though, I have to believe in others…
and this means that I must visit them and meet them –
not just casually in the hairdresser's, or the pub, or the office or factory, or on the doorstep,
where all we do is gossip about other people, or talk about the weather, the mess the government's making, the way prices are rising…
but generously, so as to take them into my heart…
and share with them something of myself.

This is hard to do…
I have been taught to protect myself with
    my privacy…
    my shyness…
    my self-imposed loneliness…
    my property.

If only I can take the risk
    to be open to others…
    to be patient with them…
    to waste time with them…
    to listen to them,
then I shall learn to believe in them, and they to believe in me.

This takes time… more even than three months… and love…
but the reward is God himself… for God is love.

Teach me, Lord, to give myself generously for others.

The Birth of Our Lord

JOSEPH went to the city of David called Bethlehem, to be registered with Mary, to whom he was engaged and who was expecting a child. While they were there, the time came for her to deliver her child. And she gave birth to her firstborn son and wrapped him in bands of cloth, and laid him in a manger, because there was no place for them in the inn. In that region there were shepherds living in the fields, keeping watch over their flock by night. Then an angel of the Lord stood before them, and said to them, "To you is born this day in the city of David a Saviour, who is the Messiah, the Lord. This will be a sign for you: you will find a child wrapped in bands of cloth and lying in a manger." And suddenly there was with the angel a multitude of the heavenly host, praising God and saying, "Glory to God in the highest heaven, and on earth peace among those whom he favours!" The shepherds said to one another, "Let us go now to Bethlehem and see this thing that has taken place, which the Lord has made known to us." So they went with haste and found Mary and Joseph, and the child lying in the manger. The shepherds returned, glorifying and praising God for all they had heard and seen, as it had been told them.

> The Word became flesh,
> and lived among us.

from Luke 2:1-20; John 1:14

Every birth is truly a miracle. Each birth marks God's entry into the world. A new-born child is made in the image of God, he is made for God, and he is only fully alive when he knows God as his Father in heaven.

This birth is the perfect sign that God is with us.
God has spoken.
His Word has been given to the world.

This is a mystery to ponder…
    a wonder to marvel at…
    a glory to sing about.
"Glory to God in the highest, and peace to his people on earth."

It scarcely seems credible that this child,
    born in such simplicity…
    recognised by only a handful of shepherds…
should be Saviour… Son of God… God-with-us…
    the Image of the invisible God…
    the last revelation of God to man.

But so he is.

I need to understand that God reveals himself to the poor and
simple…
that it is the ordinary things of life –
    a smile, a word;
    forgiveness, freedom;
    life itself and the whole of creation –
which show the grandeur of God…
that it is because he was born in poverty and simplicity that I
have the courage to approach him, for he is like me in all
things except sin.

Many of my friends are searching for God, but perhaps I do
not show them where to look for him, or how to recognise
him. Unwittingly I may have become a barrier to their faith,
    by my unwillingness to talk about God…
    by my ignorance of the Gospel message…
    by my empty materialism.

What my friends are looking for is often so simple… so
ordinary… and so human,
    that I have not grasped that their search is truly
    for God, the Word made flesh.

Let me try to become a better witness to God's presence,
    to see him in the world he has made…
    to meet him in my brothers and sisters…
    to know him through his eternal Word…
and so to proclaim him by my daily living.

        May Christ be born in me today.

The Presentation

MARY and Joseph brought Jesus up to Jerusalem to present him to the Lord. When they brought in the child Jesus to do for him what was customary under the Law, Simeon took him into his arms and praised God saying:

> "My eyes have seen your salvation,
> which you have prepared in the presence of all peoples,
> a light for revelation to the Gentiles
> and for glory to your people Israel."

Then Simeon blessed them and said to his mother Mary, "This child is destined for the falling and the rising of many in Israel, and to be a sign that will be opposed – and a sword will pierce your own soul too."

> The true light that enlightens everyone
> was coming into the world.
> He came to what was his own
> and his own people did not accept him.

from Luke 2:22-35; John 1:9,11

All belongs to God. He is the Creator. Everything comes from him and in due course returns to him. "Every good and perfect gift comes from above, from the Father of all light." Mary and Joseph knew that their wonderful gift was from God… and must be brought back to him. Simeon saw that the child would dispel the world's darkness… though through suffering and rejection.

What child is this?
His parents could not see into the future…
    could not know the life he would lead…
    or the death he would suffer…
    could not imagine the richness of the one in their care.

They knew he was called by God,
and so they did for him what God's Law required.

Of any infant we may ask, "What child is this?"
We can never fathom the mystery of another…
    or know his future…
    or map his journey.

All we know for certain is that he is called by God and that we
who have care for him must do as God's law requires.

We may learn from God:
    "When you were a child I loved you.
    I myself taught you to walk,
    I took you in my arms;
    I led you with reins of kindness,
    with leading-strings of love."
This is the Law… to love.

What is God's plan for me?
    "In God's plan
    every single person is called upon to grow.
    Each life is a vocation.
    From birth, each one of us carries within
    the seeds of personal growth.
    Each one of us can bear the fruit
    proposed for us by God."

Like Christ, I am called to enlighten the world, and so must
be ready,
    to be rejected…
    to be misunderstood…
    to suffer hardship for justice's sake…
    to be without honour among my own people.

I must first be pruned… bear much fruit… and so return to
God enriched.

O Lord be praised for what I am, and what I may become!

The Finding in the Temple

NOW every year his parents went to Jerusalem for the festival of the Passover. And when he was twelve years old, they went up as usual for the festival. When the festival was ended and they started to return, the boy Jesus stayed behind in Jerusalem, but his parents did not know it. After three days they found him in the temple, sitting among the teachers, listening to them and asking them questions. And all who heard him were amazed at his understanding and his answers. When his parents saw him they were astonished; and his mother said to him, "Child, why have you treated us like this? Look, your father and I have been searching for you in great anxiety." He said to them, "Why were you searching for me? Did you not know that I must be in my Father's house?" But they did not understand what he said to them. Then he went down with them and came to Nazareth, and was obedient to them. His mother treasured all these things in her heart. And Jesus increased in wisdom and in years, and in divine and human favour.   *Luke 2:41-43, 46-52*

At first sight the incident is inexplicable.
It is uncharacteristic… it seems to show thoughtlessness and even selfishness. But perhaps it can help me to realise how necessary it is

to let another grow…
to encourage him to be independent…
to give her room to be free…
to offer care without constraint…
to understand commitment to what is important…
to be ready always to listen to the questions being asked.

Jesus was a boy. Like all young people he needed to know himself… to find himself… and to become in his humanity what his Father was calling him to be. "Did you not know that I must be busy with my Father's affairs?… My meat is to do the will of my Father in heaven."

He listened and questioned.
There is a model for me.

What are the right questions for me to ask? Even to know the questions, I must first listen to God
   in prayer…
   in the words of Scripture…
   in the Church's teaching…
   in the advice of God's friends…
   in the wonders of his creation…
   in the voice of conscience.
As I listen, so I shall learn to question well.

Jesus grew "in wisdom, in stature, and in favour with God and men."
This is my ambition, too – to grow.
Let me realise that
while God gives the increase,
I myself have a part to play
so that growth may be possible.

I need
   to be open to the Holy Spirit, so I may repent and be
      converted…
   to take proper care of myself, so I may have the energy to
      do God's work…
   to be willing to know others, so I may meet the risen,
      living Christ…
   to take time to ponder God's Word, so I may learn true
wisdom.

Then I will come to know myself… to find myself… and to become what the Father is calling me to be.

Lord, give me the patience to grow.

THE SORROWFUL MYSTERIES

The Agony in the Garden

JESUS came out and went, as was his custom, to the Mount of Olives; and the disciples followed him. When he reached the place, he said to them, "Pray that you may not come into the time of trial." Then he withdrew from them about a stone's throw, knelt down, and prayed, "Father, if you are willing, remove this cup from me; yet, not my will but yours be done." Then an angel from heaven appeared to him and gave him strength. In his anguish he prayed more earnestly, and his sweat became like great drops of blood falling down on the ground. When he got up from prayer, he came to the disciples and found them sleeping because of grief, and he said to them, "Why are you sleeping? Get up and pray that you may not come into the time of trial."

Luke 22:39-46

Why didn't Jesus escape from his enemies? Was there any
need for him to go through all this? Could he not have left
quietly until the commotion had died down? This is the
temptation that comes to us all at one time or another:
to avoid the issue…
to choose the easy way out…
to run away from what is right…

But there are some problems that simply have to be faced.
The cup has to be drained… the burden must be carried…
the needs of others must take first place.

Jesus, like us, prayed that he could be spared… he was in an
agony of apprehension and fear so that he sweated blood.
His prayer was answered: "Not my will, but yours be done."

In my agony, let this become my prayer.

In the agony
of frustration when it seems there is nothing I can do to
ease the situation…
of being misunderstood, when it's as if the whole world
has turned its back on me…
of shame, when my sins and failures overshadow the whole
of life…
of anxiety, when my responsibilities seem too great for me
to bear…
of apprehension, when the oncoming horror is too
dreadful for me to face…
of sadness, when someone I love turns against me and
friendship dies…

Indeed I may pray not be to be put to the test, and to be
spared from such pain. But there are times when
as a result of sin…
or error…

or accident…
or sickness…
of because of human weakness and limitation…
or because of what my neighbour needs,
I shall undergo a fearful agony.

Then may I pray that I can know and accept God's will.

Lord, the Spirit is willing, but the flesh is weak!

The Scourging at the Pillar

PILATE said to the chief priests and the elders, "What should I do with Jesus who is called the Messiah?" All of them said, "Let him be crucified!" Then he asked, "Why, what evil has he done?" But they shouted all the more, "Let him be crucified!" So when Pilate saw that he could do nothing, but rather that a riot was beginning, he took some water and washed his hands before the crowd, saying, "I am innocent of this man's blood; see to it yourselves." After flogging Jesus, he handed him over to be crucified.

from Matthew 27:21-26

When people are frightened there is no depth to which they won't sink. The chief priests were frightened because
    Jesus was prepared to take the law into his own hands:
    "the sabbath was made for man, not man for the sabbath"…
    Jesus was popular with the ordinary people: "his teaching
        made a deep impression on them because, unlike the
        scribes, he taught them with authority"…

Pilate was frightened because
    Jesus was an enigma, whose kingdom was "not of this
        world"…

Jesus bore witness to the truth, and the truth is
uncomfortable for those whose lives are a lie...

So the Jewish leaders demanded his death, and Pilate looked
for a compromise.

"He has done nothing that deserves death, so I shall have him
flogged"... a sop to the Establishment... a ruthless
injustice... "it is expedient that one man should die for the
people".

How often are we prepared to allow an injustice because
it is too much trouble to do anything about it...
we don't have the power to effect a worthwhile change...
we accept the law as our first obligation...
we are afraid to accept the truth...
material affairs outweigh the spiritual.
We pass by on the other side of the road, and avert our eyes.

Let me remember the pain endured by so many of my
brothers and sisters,
the silence of the abused...
the terror of the tortured...
the innocent victims of war...
the distress of the sick...
the suffering of the handicapped...
the timidity of the lonely...
the anguish of the starving...
the heartache of the homeless...
the emptiness of the sad...
the despair of the falsely imprisoned...
They look for me – for
my presence... my friendship... my understanding...
my comforting... my bread... my generosity...
my forgiveness... my help... my respect...
a share in my happiness, joy and faith.

"Behold, the man!"

Jesus, the suffering one,
is present in all those who suffer,
and I, if I have faith, have the power to heal them.

Lord, give me the strength to bind up broken hearts.

The Crowning with Thorns

THEN the soldiers of the governor took Jesus into the governor's headquarters, and they gathered the whole cohort around him. They stripped him and put a scarlet robe on him, and after twisting some thorns into a crown, they put it on his head. They put a reed in his right hand and knelt before him and mocked him, saying, "Hail, King of the Jews!" They spat on him, and took the reed and struck him on the head.

Matthew 27:27-30

Mockery is often more hurtful than the hurt that attends it.

When Jesus Christ was yet a child,
He had a garden small and wild,
Wherein he cherished roses fair,
And wove them into garlands there.

Now once, as summer-time drew nigh,
There came a troop of children by,
And seeing roses on the tree,
With shouts they plucked them merrily.

'Do you bind roses in your hair?'
They cried, in scorn, to Jesus there.
The boy said humbly: 'Take, I pray,
All but the naked thorns away.'

> Then of the thorns they made a crown,
> And with rough fingers pressed it down,
> Till on his forehead fair and young
> Red drops of blood like roses sprung.
>
> *Plechtcheev*

I know it's not a perfect world and that envy, jealousy and hatred can be found everywhere:

> a sour suspicion born of fear that the other one is finer…
> a subtle knowledge canker-grown that the stranger's path is straighter…
> a numb awareness vainly fought that the weaker one's my leader…

These, maybe, are the thorns in my crown.

But I have a crown of roses too… as well as thorns.
My crown is woven of

> my friends, whose constancy and love urge me to generosity…
> my faith, a grace from God which tugs at me to know him…
> my forgiveness, a sign of God's love that confirms my hope…

Wearing such a crown I may learn

> to soften the thorns of selfishness…
> to be happy with the gifts I have received…
> to rejoice in the talents and success of others.

> "Glory to God in the highest,
> and peace to his people on earth."

The Carrying of the Cross

THEN Pilate handed Jesus over to the Jews to be crucified. So they took Jesus; and carrying the cross by himself, he went out to what is called The Place of the Skull, which in Hebrew is called Golgotha. As they led him away, they seized a man, Simon of Cyrene, who was coming from the country, and they laid the cross on him, and made him carry it behind Jesus. A great number of the people followed him, and among them were women who were beating their breasts and wailing for him. But Jesus turned to them and said, "Daughters of Jerusalem, do not weep for me, but weep for yourselves and for your children."

John 19:17; Luke 23:26-28

This was Jesus' last pilgrimage. His life had been marked by journeys:

    the flight to Egypt…

    the visit as a child to Jerusalem…

    and later his missionary journeys to all parts of Palestine
        to tell his fellow countrymen about his Father.

Calvary was to be the final staging post.

He had told his followers,

    "Take up your cross daily and follow me"…

    "Come to me all you who labour and are overburdened,
        and I will refresh you"…

"My yoke is easy and my burden light."

It is said that the condemned prisoner carried only the crosspiece, which was lashed to his arms… the vertical post stayed in position at the top of the hill.

The horizontal – a reminder
>   that like Christ I am on a pilgrim journey…
>   that like Christ I cannot always choose the way…
>   that like Christ I carry with me a burden I cannot lose…

The vertical – a reminder
>   that God is always there…
>   that all I do is in the end to give him glory…
>   that my journey to heaven must be rooted in the ground…

If my life is really a pilgrimage to God, carrying the weight of
myself, it is sensible
>   to abandon unnecessary trifles so as not to be encumbered,
>   for I cannot serve God and material things…
>   to be willing to lay the axe to the root of the tree and to be
>   converted,
>   for to be perfect is to have changed often…
>   to accept the company of others, their consolation and
>   their help,
>   for on my own I am powerless…

The road is rough and the falls are many.

God draws me towards himself, for
>   his love is always patient…
>   my baptism has marked me out for him…
>   my heart knows no rest until it rests in him.

Lord, see that I do not follow the wrong path
and lead me to the path of eternal life.

The Crucifixion

WHEN they came to the place that is called The Skull, they crucified Jesus there with the criminals, one on his right and one on his left. Then Jesus said, "Father, forgive them; for they do not know what they are doing." And they cast lots to divide his clothing. When it was noon, darkness came over the whole land until three in the afternoon. At three o'clock Jesus cried out with a loud voice, "My God, my God, why have you forsaken me?" Then he said, "Father, into your hands I commend my spirit." Having said this, he breathed his last. When the centurion saw what had taken place, he praised God and said, "Certainly this man was innocent." And when all the crowds who had gathered there for this spectacle saw what had taken place, they returned home, beating their breasts. But all his acquaintances, including the women who had followed him from Galilee, stood at a distance, watching these things.

Luke 23:33-34, 46-49; Mark 15:33-34

Death is inescapable, but this does not make it any less frightening. Jesus himself was afraid, and even felt for a time that he had been forgotten by his Father. There can be no worse horror than believing ourselves to have been abandoned. Such an experience can come to anyone, when
God, and faith in God seem to have vanished…
friends stand at a distance, and don't want to know us…
all those we have relied on for support suddenly have
nothing to offer…

At moments like this I must remind myself that dying should be a daily experience if the last enemy, death itself, is to be conquered.

Jesus said:

> "Unless the wheat grain falls on the ground and dies it
>   remains only a single grain,
> but if it dies,
> it yields a rich harvest…
> Anyone who finds his life will lose it;
> anyone who loses his life for my sake will find it…"

If I am to learn the art of living, I must practise the art of dying. "Death is swallowed up in victory"… it is a threshold to new life.

To die is to let go
>   of prejudices, vanities and my own opinion…
>   of those ambitions that turn me from what is worthwhile…
>   of the things, the comforts and even the people who
>   distract me from God…

To die is to become obedient
>   to God's commandments…
>   to the needs of others…
>   to the demands of the present moment…

To die is to empty myself
>   to belong to others…
>   to cast aside the inessential…
>   to leave something to God…
>   to abandon myself: "Father, into your hands I commit
>   my spirit."

At death there are no more tomorrows… but only a memory of yesterdays… and an eternal present.

Then I shall truly know that God has not forgotten me, and that I am safe in his hands.

> Lord, teach me how to die.

THE GLORIOUS MYSTERIES

The Resurrection

O N THE first day of the week, at early dawn, they came to the tomb, taking the spices that they had prepared. They found the stone rolled away from the tomb, but when they went in, they did not find the body. While they were perplexed about this, suddenly two men in dazzling clothes stood beside them. The women were terrified and bowed their faces to the ground, but the men said to them, "Why do you look for the living among the dead? He is not here, but has risen. Remember how he told you, while he was still in Galilee, that the Son of Man must be handed over to sinners, and be crucified, and on the third day rise again." Then they remembered his words.

Luke 24:1-8

The apostles were, to our way of thinking, slow to believe the full message of the Gospel. "Did you not know", the risen Christ said to the despondent couple on the road to Emmaus, "that the Christ had to suffer and so enter into his glory?"

> Wake up from your sleep
> rise from the dead
> and Christ will shine on you!

He died,
> so that his Father might raise him to a new life…
> so that all of us could be brought alive in Christ.

St Paul says, "If Christ is not risen our faith is in vain."
Let me notice the small reminders in my ordinary life that point the way to a richer life with God… and give thanks to him for
> the simple pleasure of food and drink…
> the security of shelter and home…
> the tranquillity of sleep and quiet…

Let me appreciate the emergence of new life that is a daily miracle for all its frequency and inevitability… and praise God for
> the coming to birth of a new day…
> the beauty produced by the work of human hands…
> the recovery of strength after sickness…
> and, above all, the birth of a child…

Let me marvel at the brief resurrections I experience in my struggle to follow Christ… and thank God for
> forgiveness, after failure and sin…
> praise, when all I had expected was to be unnoticed…
> trust, when I knew it was undeserved…
> welcome, in spite of my selfish isolation.

All of this is an anticipation and promise of what is to come… which eye has not seen… nor ear heard… which has not entered into our hearts.

If I want to be alive I must "eat the flesh of the Son of Man and drink his blood"… I must do as he did… in memory of him. My communion with him at Mass is the perfect foretaste of what is to come and the source of the resurrection I must search for:

That Sacred Banquet
in which Christ is received…
the memory of his Passion recalled…
the mind filled with grace…
and a pledge of future glory given.

"Lord, that I may live, and live to the full!"

The Ascension

I PRAY that the God of our Lord Jesus Christ, the Father of glory, may give you a spirit of wisdom and revelation as you come to know him, so that, with the eyes of your heart enlightened, you may know what is the hope to which he has called you, what are the riches of his glorious inheritance among the saints, and what is the immeasurable greatness of his power for us who believe, according to the working of his great power. God put this power to work in Christ when he raised him from the dead and seated him at his right hand in the heavenly places, far above all rule and authority and power and dominion, and above every name that is named, not only in this age but also in the age to come. And he has put all things under his feet and has made him the head over all things for the church, which is his body, the fullness of him who fills all in all.

Jesus came and said to them, "All authority in heaven and on earth has been given to me. Go therefore and make disciples of all nations, baptizing them in the name of the Father and of the

Son and of the Holy Spirit, and teaching them to obey everything that I have commanded you. And remember, I am with you always, to the end of the age."

Ephesians 1:17-23; Matthew 28:18-20

Jesus is now with his Father… continually interceding on our behalf. But he is alive too in all the members of his Body, the Church… he fills them with his own life… he encourages, forgives, guides… he helps the whole of creation to achieve its purpose.

The Master Craftsman has given his apprentices all he can… it is for them now, under his care, to continue his work… to witness… to heal… to set free those who are enslaved. Much has been entrusted to us.

I'm scared of such great responsibility:
    "You can't mean me to do this, Lord"…
    "Lord, I am not worthy"…
    "I do not know how to speak, Lord: I'm only a child"…

I want to hide and leave it to those who are better fitted: the bishops… the priests… the nuns… the clever ones… the holy ones. And all he says to me is
    "Do not be afraid, for I have redeemed you…
    I have called you by your name…
    and you are mine."

I am part of the Body of Christ… there are all sorts of service to be done… but it is the same God who is working in all of them… I cannot say "Christ has no need of me"… my place, my work, my mission are indispensable… I need not be fainthearted, because Jesus Christ is working in me… with him all things are possible.

I must be ready, then, to be a witness to the power of Christ in me

by hearing his word and keeping it…
by making his teaching my own…
by spreading the Gospel by word and action…
by practising justice and integrity…
by readiness to take up my cross daily…
by faithfulness to my daily prayer…

If he is on my side… I have nothing to fear.

My witness may be silent… but it will be none the less strong and effective.

> "O Lord, open my lips;
> and my tongue shall announce your praise!"

The Coming of the Holy Spirit

I WILL ask the Father, and he will give you another Advocate, to be with you forever. The Advocate, the Holy Spirit, whom the Father will send in my name, will teach you everything, and remind you of all that I have said to you.

When the day of Pentecost had come, they were all together in one place. And suddenly from heaven there came a sound like the rush of a violent wind, and it filled the entire house where they were sitting. Divided tongues, as of fire, appeared among them, and a tongue rested on each of them. All of them were filled with the Holy Spirit and began to speak in other languages, as the Spirit gave them ability.

John 14:16, 26; 14:23; Acts 2:1-4

God's mystery is gradually unfolded. He is Father… Creator… the one who holds all things in being… Shepherd of his people… Bridegroom.

He is Son… the Son of God made man… the Word made flesh… the image of the invisible God… who died so that we might live.

He is Holy Spirit… sent by the Father and the Son… Advocate… Helper… Breath of Life… who comes to everyone who invites him. The Spirit of God is our partner… who ennobles… teaches… directs.

The gifts of the Spirit cannot be counted… there are as many gifts as there are people in the world, and more besides… but among them we can number –
   the wisdom of those who know true worth…
   the understanding of a mother who can reach her child's
      heart…
   the judgement of the youngster who reads a situation with
      uncomplicated simplicity…
   the courage of the one prepared to swim against the
      stream…
   the knowledge of the person of prayer, whose faith and
      peace are unshakeable…
   the unfathomable respect of a son for his father, and of a
      father for his son…
   the cheerfulness of the dying… the generosity of the
      poor… the angry fire of the prophet… the patience of
      the teacher… the smile of a friend… the sorrow of a
      sinner… the compassion of the one who forgives…
      the joy of the one forgiven.

The disciples of Jesus were dispirited… they had lost heart… the bottom had dropped out of their lives… the urgency of the Gospel had disappeared… they were filled with fear. "What can we do?"… "Is God still with us?"… "What will happen to us?"…

Then the Spirit came and all was changed. They were enlivened… inspired… encouraged… renewed. They were eager with the fire of unselfish love… alive with the rhythm of a new beginning… confident in the discovery of truth.

I must look for my personal Pentecost… always ready to accept God's Spirit… willing to be converted… happy to abandon myself to the Spirit's urgent leadership… so that there may grow in me the Christian instinct for truth… love… joy… peace… patience… kindness… goodness… trustfulness… gentleness… self-control.

"Come, O Holy Spirit and kindle in me
the fire of your love."

The Assumption

CHRIST has been raised from the dead, the first fruits of those who have died. For since death came through a human being, the resurrection of the dead has also come through a human being; for as all die in Adam, so all will be made alive in Christ. But each in his own order: Christ the first fruits, then at his coming those who belong to Christ.

But God, who is rich in mercy, out of the great love with which he loved us even when we were dead through our trespasses, made us alive together with Christ—by grace you have been saved – and raised us up with him and seated us with him in the heavenly places in Christ Jesus, so that in the ages to come he might show the immeasurable riches of his grace in kindness toward us in Christ Jesus. For by grace you have been saved through faith, and this is not your own doing; it is the gift of God – not the result of works, so that no one may boast. For we are what he has made us, created in Christ Jesus for good works, which God prepared beforehand to be our way of life.

1 Corinthians 15:20-23; Ephesians 2:4-10

In a very special way Mary is God's work of art.
Alone of creation she lived the good life
as from the beginning she was called by God to live it.

Like all works of art she was irreplaceable… indestructible…
incorruptible. She was unscathed and untouched by the sin of
the world that she lived in… she knew not sin… and so
conquered the one who fathers death.

> Mary immaculate, star of the morning,
> chosen before the creation began,
> chosen to bring, for your bridal adorning,
> woe to the serpent and rescue to man.

She was chosen to be
> the mother of the Lord… who would triumph over sin and
> death;
> the second Eve… bringing not death but life;
> the new mother of Mankind… taking all into her heart.

After her Son – "the first-fruits of all who have fallen asleep"
– she was brought to life in Christ. It was by God's grace that
she was saved, for all are given life by God's free gift.

She was full of grace… supremely free to choose… wholly
willing to walk the passage of earthly life to the incomparable
life of glory.

In my daily life I have
> to struggle against temptation…
> to endure the suffering that comes to everyone…
> to bring woe to the serpent and rescue to my neighbour…
> to be able to say "Amen" to God's will for me…
> to learn the secrets of the good life to which I am called.

But by God's grace I am what I am… his grace is sufficient
for me… he never allows me to be tempted beyond my
strength… he offers me unbounded grace, real freedom,
strength and companionship.

Like Mary I am invited to bring forth Christ to the world… to share God's life… to be with him… to live as from the beginning he meant me to live.

And all is gift.

> "Grace has brought me safe thus far,
> and grace will lead me home."

Our Lady, Queen of Heaven

STANDING near the cross of Jesus was his mother. When Jesus saw his mother and the disciple whom he loved standing beside her, he said to his mother, "Woman, here is your son." Then he said to the disciple, "Here is your mother." And from that hour the disciple took her into his own home.

After this I looked, and there was a great multitude that no one could count, from every nation, from all tribes and peoples and languages, standing before the throne and before the Lamb, robed in white, with palm branches in their hands. They cried out in a loud voice, saying, "Salvation belongs to our God who is seated on the throne, and to the Lamb!" And all the angels stood around the throne and around the elders and the four living creatures, and they fell on their faces before the throne and worshipped God, singing, "Amen! Blessing and glory and wisdom and thanksgiving and honour and power and might be to our God forever and ever! Amen."

John 19:25-27; Revelation 7:9-12

The picture I may have of heaven need not bother me. I know I cannot even begin to imagine it and that no language can describe it for me. It is enough to appreciate the promise of the past and the reality of present hope.

The past is made by those who have gone before,
> the great men and women who lived before Christ, in hope for his coming...
> the mother of Christ, who was blessed because she believed in God's promise...
> the apostles and disciples of Jesus, who came to believe that he was the Promised One...
> the Christian saints, who have heard the Word of God and kept it...
> the men and women of good will, who have searched for what is right and good and have found God.

To these, "a number impossible to count", the risen Lord has already said: "Come you blessed of my Father, into the kingdom prepared for you from the foundation of the world." The Word of God was sown in them and they brought forth good fruit.

Mary is their queen,
> the mother who belongs to all, because she gave her Son to the world...
> the daughter who gives courage to all, because of God's faithfulness to her...
> the virgin who gives hope to all, because of the fruitfulness of her poverty...
> the woman who brings comfort to all, because she believed and was saved...

What is my present hope?
> that God is with me, cares for me, guides me, loves me, and asks me to make my home with him...

that he has given me, for the time being, charge of the
    world he made, to help me grow in wisdom and grace…

that he has placed me in a world peopled by other men
    and women, my brothers and sisters, so that together
    we may love and serve him…

that his friends who have lived in this world before me,
    among them especially Mary, the mother of God, are
    my friends too…

that together we belong to God and to one another, and
    are in communion of mind, heart and soul…

With such a hope, I am indeed greatly blessed.

> "Pray for me, a sinner,
> now and at the hour of my death.
> Amen."

A Meditation on the Beatitudes

"Be perfect
as your heavenly Father
is perfect."

Lord I hear you say,
"Be perfect as your heavenly Father is perfect",
and I am afraid.
I cannot do what you ask;
you don't expect me to be like God himself?
You know, Lord, that I can never be perfect.
Why do you ask me then even to try?

Perhaps you can't be perfect yet,
but you can always grow.
So set your sights high,
don't refuse to walk a bit further,
or say you have no more to give.

Never be anxious about your weaknesses;
always know that I will give you strength;
try to forgive even those who don't forgive you;
learn what it is to be free;
try not to think evil of others;
be compassionate towards your fellows;
be generous and unstinted in your love;
live from moment to moment
without worrying about tomorrow.

You can always walk this step,
and this step is the only one that matters.
To be perfect is not to have achieved all,
but to put no limits to your giving,
to draw no horizon to what is possible,
never to say, "Thus far and no further".

If you can become like that
you will learn what it is like to be like God.

So here is a pattern for your living
– your generous living –
that will bring you true and lasting happiness:

- Blessed are the poor in spirit,
  for theirs is the kingdom of heaven.

- Blessed are those who mourn,
  for they will be comforted.

- Blessed are the meek,
  for they will inherit the earth.

- Blessed are those who hunger and thirst for
    righteousness,
  for they will be filled.

- Blessed are the merciful,
  for they will receive mercy.

- Blessed are the pure in heart,
  for they will see God.

- Blessed are the peacemakers,
  for they will be called children of God.

- Blessed are those who are persecuted for
    righteousness' sake,
  for theirs is the kingdom of heaven.

REJOICE AND BE GLAD, for your reward is great in heaven,
for in the same way they persecuted the prophets who were
before you.

Matthew 5:2-10

Help me, Lord, to accept this demanding law,
that completes the law of Sinai.
Help me not to be angry with my brother or sister,
not to lust with my mind and heart after another,
to speak the truth,
to be honest and sincere,
to offer good in return for evil,
to give to those who ask,
to trust in your goodness and care,
and to praise and thank you always. Amen.

"Blessed are the poor in spirit, for theirs is the kingdom of heaven."

There are times, Lord, when I know how poor I really am.
I know that without you I have nothing and I am nothing,
    and I am happy in this knowledge.
But these times are rare.
More often, in my pride, I try to live alone –
I forget you and ignore my friends.

> Even if you forget me,
> I shall never forget you,
> because I love you
> as tenderly as a mother loves her child.
> To be poor is just to let me be with you,
> to empty yourself of the rubbish in your life,
> so that there is room for me.
> I promise that you will never then be in need
> of the things that really count.
> Learn to be content with who you are,
> to be able to live with your failings,
> to be glad about your strengths,
> to rejoice in the goodness of others.
> This is humility,
> this is poverty.
> Be like the child
> who is generous in giving and receiving,
> who is glad to be everyone's friend.
> Poverty is a good platform for friendship.

Lord, what of the good things of life,
of food and drink, of money, security and property?
How can I have these
and still deserve the reward of the poor?

> These are gifts,
> and every good gift comes from me.
> It is how you use them that is important –
> do you use them for yourself or for others?
> Accept the things of creation
> and the work of human hands
> gladly and responsibly.
> Be honest and generous,
> share with those in need,
> give open-handedly and without anxiety.
> Give of yourself —
> your time, your skill, your enthusiasm,
> your kindness, your forgiveness, your compassion.
> Let go, empty yourself, surrender yourself to me,
> then surely you will discover one day
> the pearl of great price,
> and will be at peace.

———————————

Lord, if at times I try to serve two masters,
be patient with me.
Teach me to recognise what is of real value
and not to worry about success, praise or material reward.
Plant in me the seed of poverty
so that one day I may hear your call
to leave all things and follow you. Amen.

"Blessed are those who mourn, for they will be comforted."

I'm not sure, Lord,
whether my sadness is true mourning,
or just self-pity and depression.
I'm ashamed of my failures,
scared of being hurt,
afraid that I'll be punished for my sins,
overwhelmed when I realise what you are asking of me.

> I was afraid too, you know.
> It's human to be scared or overwhelmed,
> but try not to be afraid of being human,
> and remember always that you are loved
> with a tremendous love.
> The things that worry you
> – your shame, self-anger and fear –
> are only dangerous if that is where you stop.
> I'm asking you to look beyond yourself
> towards God, your Father, who loves you
> and asks for your love and trust;
> and towards the whole company of your fellow men
> and women
> with their problems and anxieties –
> they too ask for your love and trust.
> Love God and love your neighbour as yourself.
>
> Mourn for your sinfulness and failure
> because you have been less than you are capable of
> being,
> less than what God has called you to be,

and so have weakened the bond of fellowship.
Your generous, unselfish sorrow,
that accepts responsibility
and seeks forgiveness from your Father
and from your brothers and sisters,
will indeed be comforted.
No one can refuse unselfish sorrow.

Mourn, too, with those who suffer:
with the sick, the lonely and depressed,
with the anxious and those who have no friends,
with the apparent failures of the world.
Be aware of them, care for them as best you can,
suffer with them, pray with them, weep with them.
Such real compassion brings its own reward,
of acceptance, trust and healing.
Give, and there will be gifts for you:
a full measure,
pressed down, shaken together, and running over,
will be poured into your lap;
because the amount you measure out
is the amount you will be given back.

Lord, help me to see myself
as a true member of your family,
and to know that others depend on me
as I do on them.
Bring me to a self-forgetful sorrow,
and to an unsparing compassion,
so that in learning to mourn
I may discover the comfort of your presence. Amen.

"Blessed are the meek for they will inherit the earth."

Meek, Lord? What does it mean?

If you think of those who aren't meek
you'll see its meaning clearly enough.
The sharp person who trades in unkind words;
the perfectionist who finds fault in everything;
the boaster who never listens to others;
the jealous person who is afraid of your cleverness;
the authoritarian who plays everything by the rule book;
the older man or woman who damps the fire of your
  enthusiasm;
the younger person who is impatient of your slowness,
These sad people inherit bitterness, loneliness and fear;
they stand on their own platform and cut themselves off
from others.

To be meek is to have discovered a quiet strength.
Learn of me for I am meek and humble of heart.

Tame yourself,
find the balance of your life,
look for the strength of self-control.
Know that anger can be a gift –
not the violence of unbridled and selfish passion,
but the force that impels you to right what is wrong.

If you are corrected for wrong-doing
accept the reproach without seeking to justify yourself;
do not look for revenge;
be courteous towards your accusers.

Use the power you have
to set people free, and not to enslave;
blow gently on the smouldering flax;
be ready with praise and speak generously of others.

Listen sympathetically to excuses;
accept an apology unhesitatingly;
try to understand the other person's feelings;
be gentle towards those who are fearful;
act always with feeling care.

Appreciate the idealism of the young;
heed the wisdom of the old;
be patient with young and old alike;
listen attentively to authority.

Tamed by God,
you will inherit a world of peace,
where nothing can harm you,
and everyone is your friend.

Lord, forgive me for my unkindness –
for the harsh and thoughtless things I do and say.
Give me the grace of self-control
and the strength to be gentle,
so that, learning to be meek and humble of heart,
I may be a friend to the friendless
and a support for the weak. Amen.

"Blessed are those who hunger and thirst for righteousness, for they will be filled."

Lord, I do care about justice,
and try to act justly towards others.
I'm honest about money, and usually tell the truth;
I give a certain amount to charity.
I want people to be free and to be fully alive.
I get angry when I read of torture and cruelty,
and I deplore the dishonesty and callousness I see in
    the world.
Then I remember the parable about the pharisee and the
    publican,
and I wonder…

It is good to care about justice
and to work in whatever way you can
to bring greater freedom to the world.
But the justice I want you to practise and proclaim
is something deeper than you may yet have discovered.
Just people are those who are at rights with God and
    their fellow men and women.
They know that God loves them
and is always beckoning them to come closer;
they live with God as with a familiar friend,
confident that love covers a multitude of sins;
they know that God loved the world so much
that he sent his only Son,
so that all who believe in him would be saved.
They have learned, too, to love their enemy;

they offer the wicked no resistance;
they are quick to forgive any who have hurt them;
they give to those who ask, and lend without question.
They have set their hearts on the things of God,
content that God's gifts will bring them deep happiness.
The grace you need to pray for
is not just to care about justice,
but to be able to hunger and thirst for what is right,
to be urgent, anxious and aching to be made right by God,
to be willing to spend yourself utterly in the quest for
    righteousness.
It is the grace to speak freely with outcasts without shame,
to be prepared to see the good of others, whoever they
    may be,
to have the courage to be thought a fool for my sake,
to have a heart big enough to contain the world.

Your search for justice is your search for God.
Ask, and it will be given to you;
search, and you will find;
knock, and the door will be opened to you.

Be sure that you will have your fill:
in justifying others you yourself will be justified;
by easing another's burden you will be made free;
in leading your friend to God your own search will be
satisfied.

—————————————

Lord, you know how half-hearted I am in my search,
and how often I blind myself to what is truly right.
Forgive my lack of urgency and eagerness.
Set me on fire with your Spirit,
show me the path of justice,
and give me the vision and courage to live as your
disciple. Amen.

"Blessed are the merciful, for they will receive mercy."

Have I ever the chance, Lord, to be merciful?
Isn't this something for people with authority,
like judges, magistrates, the police, teachers or
employers?
I don't have power over others,
so how can I show mercy?

> You often ask for mercy:
> you pray, "Lord, have mercy";
> but do you realise what you are asking for?
> It should be more than a plea not to be punished,
> or for the scales of justice to be balanced in your favour.
> God is not a magistrate or an employer
> who has to apply the law rigorously
> and treat everyone according to what they deserve.
> He is your Father.
> He is full of compassion and love,
> and he has made a promise with you
> that come what may he will never disown you.
> He will not forget you or leave you;
> he will always be faithful and steadfast.
> This is his mercy –
> his promise to reach out to the poor, weak and sinful;
> so that with his free gift they may live.
> Your prayer for mercy is a reminder to God
> for him to fulfil his promise to you –
> to be compassionate, patient, forgiving, loving
> towards you.

Mercy is a truly godly quality.
It enriches the bond between you and your friends –
    and enemies.
If you would be great, practise mercy towards others.

Remember the parable about the unforgiving debtor,
who, though his own huge debt was cancelled,
demanded payment from his fellow worker –
and learn to forgive as often as you are injured.

Read the story of the latecomers to the vineyard,
who, because of the generosity of their employer,
were paid the same wages as the rest –
and discover the love that exceeds justice.

Recall the wounded man who, ignored by his friends,
was cared for by his enemy, the Samaritan –
and know that it is in deeds that mercy is shown.

In all your dealings with others,
whether as one in authority or not,
be aware of them as your companions in the Lord;
understand their strengths and weaknesses, their
    burdens and gifts;
be tolerant of their failures
as you would want them to be tolerant of yours.
Your trust in them will help them trust in you;
your faithfulness to them will encourage them to love.

Your mercy will be twice blessed:
"It blesseth him that gives, and him that takes."

Lord, be merciful to me a sinner!
Through the experience of your mercy to me
may my love for others become more generous.
May it be a practical love that responds to what is needed,
a forgiving love that does not impose conditions,
and an understanding love that sustains the weary soul.
Amen.

"Blessed are the pure in heart, for they will see God."

Lord, you search me and you know me,
you know my deepest thoughts and feelings.
So often I do those things I don't want to do,
and fail to do what in my inmost heart I eagerly desire.
I pray for purity of mind and heart and body,
yet my prayer seems unanswered.
Shall I ever see God face to face?

Your cross, which you cannot escape, is yourself.
Accept this burden gratefully and willingly,
and realise that it is a blessing for you
to be this woman or this man.
Like any cross you may want to shrug it off at times;
then come to me and you will find rest for your soul.
If you would be my disciple you must bear with yourself.
I shall not let you be tried beyond your strength.

The attraction you have for others and they for you
is something to praise God for,
not to be ashamed or frightened of.
See in it a source of your growth,
and not a threat to your immortality.

Take courage.
What is in your heart is what is most important.
It is from the heart that evil comes,
and if your heart is pure
and the spirit is willing,
then even if the flesh is weak
you shall find forgiveness and hope.

Learn, if you can, from the purity of the child.
There is in such a one a simplicity and directness
that dissolves all prejudice and anger.
The child's innocence is a light
that the darkness cannot overpower.

Children's friendship is for everyone.
Their thoughts go with uncomplicated ease
to the heart of the problem.
They are pure, untouched by evil, unadulterated.

Do not judge yourself too harshly.
Strive to be simple and sincere.
Remember the importance of a humble and contrite
    heart.
Do not be anxious about your motives,
but do straightforwardly what you see to be right.

One day your cross will be mounted like mine on
    Calvary,
so that through that final death
you may take up your new life with God.
Then you will know him face to face,
and the purity of your heart will at last triumph
over the weakness of your body.
I am the resurrection and the life;
He who believes in me will have eternal life.

Lord, when my eyes are blinded
and my ears are deafened by false attractions,
keep my heart fixed on you.
Help me to find again the sincerity and simplicity
that leads directly to you,
the object of my real desire. Amen.

"Blessed are the peacemakers, for they will be called children of God."

Lord, you can't open a newspaper or listen to the news
without learning of some new attack on peace.
There's everything — terrible atrocities,
child abuse, torture, the breakdown of marriage.
How does a follower of yours
even begin to struggle against these evils?

> Do you believe that true peace is possible,
> or do you in your heart of hearts
> think that this is an impossible dream?
>
> There is only one road to peace,
> and that is for you to be at peace in yourself
> and with your fellow men and women.
> Love your neighbour as yourself.
> Love your enemy,
> do good to those who insult you,
> pray for those who persecute and calumniate you.
>
> I came to bring peace.
> My work was to build bridges between people,
> and to span the gulf between human beings and God.
> It meant trying to break the barriers of prejudice,
> healing those who were sick in body, mind and soul,
> helping people to realise that they could be free.
> If you want to be my disciple
> this is your work too.
> Your personal peace will come with the knowledge
> that you are truly forgiven and redeemed.

My peace I leave you, my peace I give you;
a peace that is more than the ending of conflict,
rather the meeting of minds and hearts
that marks the beginning of reconciliation and
    contentment.
Your certainty that you are safe in God's hands
is what gives you the authority and power to make
    peace.

It will give you the courage to be uncompromising
in confronting violence and slavery.
It will show you the gentleness needed
in healing those hurt by evil.
It will bring you the wisdom and skill
to temper anger and remove suspicion.

You may not sway the world,
remove the threat of war,
decrease the crime rate,
or make marriage more stable.
But be sure that by your actions for peace
the world is thereby blessed.
Without your tears the ocean is the poorer.

If you make peace even in small things
you are my sister or brother,
and will share my inheritance with the Father.

Lord, give me the strength, confidence and patience
to work for a true and lasting peace.
May I find peace in my own heart,
and bring your peace to family, friends and fellow workers.
Help me to do the small things well
so that the greater may follow,
for your sake and for the world. Amen

"Blessed are those who are persecuted for righteousness' sake, for theirs is the kingdom of heaven."

I admire the martyrs, Lord, and deeply respect them,
but I'm not that sort of person.
I don't think I'd stand up to persecution,
and in any case I don't really do anything
that people would want to attack me for.

> Has anyone ever derided your faith,
> attacked your stand for Christian morality,
> or smiled at your praying?
> Do you ever deny yourself something on my account,
> suffer because people pass me by,
> or accept the pain of cross-bearing?
> If you are faithful in these things
> you are already a witness to my name,
> and in your witnessing you are a martyr.
>
> If you live up to your Christian calling
> you are certain, sooner or later, to be persecuted.
> As my disciple you will slowly learn to be different,
> to be a sign of contradiction to those
> who worship other gods.
> Your standards will rebuke the world,
> so that your own people will disown you.
> Even by your silence you will confront others
> and risk their anger and contempt.
> You will be in the world, but not of it.

As a member of my own Body
I invite you to speak on my behalf –
boldly, in season and out of season, to prophesy.
I ask you to take your part, by word and action,
in preaching the truth my Father has revealed,
to a world that is hungry for truth.

Embrace this truth yourself;
live according to the truth;
proclaim the truth with conviction;
share the truth willingly.
You can be confident, for I am with you.
I shall send you the Spirit of truth
who will teach you all things
and fill you with the fire of his love.
And the truth will set you free.

When they persecute you,
teach them to love,
for perfect love casts out fear;
and forgive them,
for they know not what they do.
Rejoice and be glad,
for the suffering of the saints brings life to a fallen world.
Your reward will be great in heaven.

Lord, I pray for the grace to become a Christian.
Teach me how to live a Gospel life:
help me always to stand up for the truth,
and never to condone a lie by my inaction.
May I learn to suffer gladly for bearing your name,
so that the world may know that you have sent me,
and that your word is true. Amen.

A Meditation on the Way of the Cross

FOLLOWING Christ's Way of the Cross in prayer is of long tradition. Christian faith has always seen that to welcome and to carry the Cross is central to the Christian way of life. There are many meditations written to encourage believers, either alone or with others, to walk this Way prayerfully and reflectively as an act of faith and hope.

AN OPENING PRAYER

Lord Jesus Christ

your Way of the Cross

was the crown of your life among us.

By your death and resurrection

you have won new life for us,

and given us new hope.

We pray that

by walking this Way with you

we may come to know, serve

and follow you more closely,

today and every day.

Amen.

IN THE NAME OF THE FATHER

AND OF THE SON

AND OF THE HOLY SPIRIT.

AMEN.

THE FIRST STATION

Jesus is condemned to death

Condemnation

The play-acting that has been taking place is a
perfect example of the weak-minded judge.

Pilate is frightened –
of the Jews, of Caesar, of Christ.

The hand-washing is the crowning sign
of his weakness.

He had power, but would have had no power at all
were it not given from above.

"Do not judge so that you may not be judged."

Matthew 7:1

Yet I often judge others…
sometimes needlessly and rashly.

Is it ever for me to judge others…
or their motives?
Can I ever do so rightly?

Perhaps sometimes I do have to make a decision about another.

Then, Lord, let me do so with real justice,
and with mercy.

Let my motive always be love…
love of God and neighbour and not of self.

Help me always to judge others
as I hope they would judge me.

Teach me to judge others
as I hope you will judge me.

THE SECOND STATION
Jesus takes up his cross

Cross-bearing

A cross is synonymous in our language with a burden...
something heavy, unwieldy, unwanted... something to get rid of.

Jesus carrying his cross has made the cross a symbol of victory.

It has become the sign in which we conquer.

We need not think of it as a burden –
"for my yoke is easy, and my burden is light".

Matthew 11:30

What is my cross?

It is first of all me with my failings, imperfections, eccentricities.

It is my fears –
   the fear of facing up to my responsibilities...
   the fear of boredom with my daily routine...
   the fear of being found out...
   the fear of what other people think of me...
   the fear of loneliness...
   the fear of failure...
   the fear of pain, sickness and death.

"Take up your cross daily, and follow me."

Luke 9:23

Jesus, I am lumbered with myself... help me to find my feet and to be at peace.

THE THIRD STATION

Jesus falls the first time

Falling

It is incredible that Jesus Christ, God made man, should fall down.

We have to remind ourselves that he was a man, "Like us in all things except sin".

He was born... was nursed like any other baby... he was subject to the same laws of nature as we are.

He ''grew and became strong, filled with wisdom; and the favour of God was upon him".

Luke 2:40

He was a man... as physically weak as all of us are... he knew his weakness: "My Father, if it is possible, let this cup pass from me..."

Matthew 26:39

Do I know my weakness?

Is part of my trouble that I think I'm stronger than I really am?

Am I too impatient in my journey towards God?

Do I stumble through over-confidence and pride?

Help me to know my weakness, Lord, so that I can overcome the petty faults which keep me from you...

> my thoughtlessness towards others...
> my slowness to praise another...
> my carelessness in prayer...
> my obstinacy in holding to my own opinion...
> my impatience and irritability.

Help me, Jesus, to learn by my mistakes, and always to lean on you.

Jesus meets his blessed mother

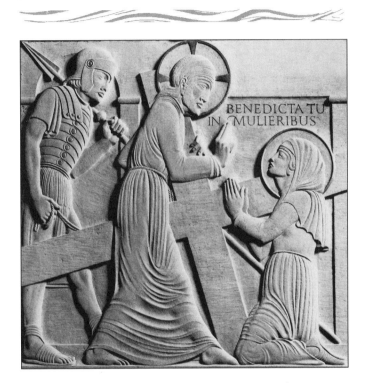

Desolation

Can we really imagine this?

The summit of a mother's selflessness –
the giving of her son.

Even if she know all that was involved it was still a loss…
    an inexpressible anguish…
    a suffering with him in perfect sympathy…
    a weight of sadness that there was so little she could
      do to help…

  yet a contentment that she could be with him and
      comfort him.

Isn't this often a mother's and a father's sorrow?
The loss, for a time, of their children… the fear that they may
have failed them?

Isn't it, too, a child's sorrow?
To be cut off from parents by petty misunderstandings…
by wanting to be free from control… by loneliness…
by feeling unwanted and not truly valued?

Young people have their own cross to carry to the top of their
own Calvary.

On the way they need the affection, sympathy, forgiveness,
security of their family –
who perhaps, like Mary, can do so little to help.

Help me, Mary, to take my cue from you…
to bear, if need be, the sight of my children leaving me…
to be with them when I'm needed…
to hide from them my own sadness.

Help me, Jesus, to be gentle with my parents…
to understand them and to forgive them…
and to let them help me.

THE FIFTH STATION
Simon of Cyrene helps Jesus to carry his cross

Sharing

What sort of a man was Simon... what did he do for a living... why was he in Jerusalem... why was he watching this sordid procession?

He was probably a very ordinary person like you or me... just in from the country for a day or two... eager to see the city sights... inquisitive for cheap entertainment.

Then he was hauled out from the crowd and forced to take part in it all.

How did he react?

Surely he was first of all angry and afraid.

This is so often my reaction when I'm pilloried in any way – anger and fear.

Angry that someone has doubted my word... afraid that perhaps I'm not right after all.

Angry because my little pedestal has been upset... afraid that I won't be able to get back on it again.

Angry with the foolishness of others who don't or won't hold the same view as me... afraid that I may be made to look more foolish than them.

Help me, Lord Jesus, to master my fear and anger, which so often stem from pride and self-love.

Help me to be glad if, even in small ways, I can share your cross.

Help me to be at peace with myself, following in your footsteps.

THE SIXTH STATION
Veronica wipes the face of Jesus

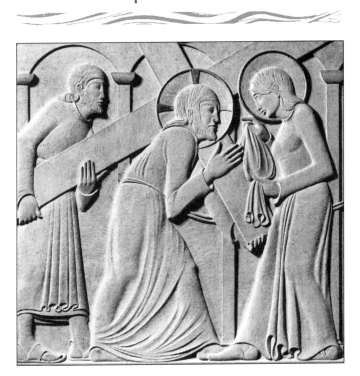

Compassion

This is a simple act of charity…
but splendidly heroic and uniquely rewarded.

I don't have the chance to perform acts like that…
Indeed, I'm foolish if I think I can.

This is part of my trouble –
I day-dream all the time…

I wonder what I would have done…
whether I would have behaved like

> Veronica…
> Simon of Cyrene…
> Peter…
> Judas…
> The soldiers…

But such wondering is fruitless.

All I need to ask is whether I do, here and now, behave like
Veronica… whether I am courageous in my giving.

If I do, the reward is the same…
I receive the imprint of Christ on my life.

"You are God's chosen race, his saints; he loves you, and you
should be clothed in sincere compassion… kindness…
humility… meekness… patience.
Bear with one another… forgive each other."

see Colossians 3

"Above all, clothe yourselves with love, which binds everything
together in perfect harmony."

Colossians 3:14

This is both the reward of our charity, and its cause.

THE SEVENTH STATION
Jesus falls the second time

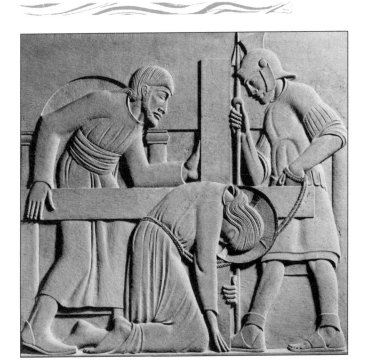

Breaking point

In the garden Jesus prayed:

"My Father, if it is possible, let this cup pass from me; yet not
what I want but what you want."

Matthew 26:39

On the cross he said:
"My God, my God, why have you forsaken me?"

Matthew 27:46

Did Jesus have difficulty on the way of the cross?
We seem to take for granted his perseverance…
his trust in his heavenly Father.
But this was genuine perseverance, genuine trust.

There is nothing sham in the humanity of Christ.

My way of the cross is pretty easy by comparison.
Yet I, too, need trust and the grace of perseverance…
and especially in the sacrament of penance.

My sins are so routine…

I have to confess the same ones again and again…
maybe I can take comfort in this…
perhaps I'm getting no worse.

I must learn to persevere in my sorrow…
to show, by my actions, that my sorrow is real…
never to let my conscience become calloused…
never to become oblivious to a fault,
     however slight it seems to be…
never to stop trying.

I must learn to trust more completely in God…
to have an unwearied hope that in the end,
     like Christ, I shall overcome.
After all, God has promised me just that.

THE EIGHTH STATION

The women of Jerusalem mourn for Jesus

Weep not...

These were kind people who were genuinely sad to see such suffering. But in spite of their sincerity and kindness they missed the point. "Was it not necessary that the Messiah should suffer these things and then enter into his glory?"

Luke 24:26

Do I mourn about the right things?
"Woe to you who are laughing now,
for you will mourn and weep."
"Blessed are you who weep now,
for you will laugh."

Luke 6:24,21

There is so much false joy in the world – escapism... irony...
facetiousness... the ridiculing of human virtue... mockery...
empty pleasure seeking.

This is only a preparation for tears.

Such sorrow can lead to misery... to bitterness... to despair...
to frustration... to the rejection of the truth... to loss of faith.

Indeed, such sorrow is without faith... or hope... or love.

In our sorrow we can always come to God... "You who weep
now, come to this God, for he is weeping." By our tears we make
up what is lacking in the sorrows of Christ. This can be the true
sorrow that leads us to joy. The joy that we are part of God's
plan, that we can share in the Incarnation... in the Redemption.

Joy is the keynote of Christian spirituality. The Gospel is the
good news of great joy. The origin of our joy is the Incarnation...
"the God who became man, that man might become God".

THE NINTH STATION
Jesus falls a third time

Collapse

We can scarcely blame the onlookers if they failed to see this is a triumphal journey. The psalmist's description is accurate enough –

But I am a worm, and not human;
> scorned by others, and despised by the people.
I am poured out like water,
> and all my bones are out of joint;
my heart is like wax;
> it is melted within my breast;

my mouth is dried up like a potsherd,
     and my tongue sticks to my jaws;
you lay me in the dust of death.

from Psalm 22

A description, in its way, of me.
Weak of will...
lax of conscience...
dry of love.
In such a state I deserve to be despised.

I need both goading and encouraging.

You speak to me, Lord, when I pray –
     encourage me to listen to you patiently.

You speak to me, Lord, when I am reading or listening to a homily –
encourage me to listen humbly... intelligently... without undue criticism. Unless I become as a little child, I shall not enter into the kingdom of heaven.

Lord, goad me to perfection.

THE TENTH STATION
Jesus is stripped of his clothes

DIVISE ... RVNT ... SIBI VES ... TIMENTA
MEA: ET ... SV ... PER ... VESTEM
MEAM ... MISE ... RVIT ... SORTEM

Naked

By way of humiliation this was the last straw.

"Who, though he was in the form of God,
did not count equality with God a thing to be exploited,
but emptied himself,
taking the form of a slave,
being born in human likeness.

And being found in human form,
he humbled himself,

and became obedient to the point of death –
even death on a cross."

Philippians 2:5-8

He did not prize his possessions,
neither those due to him as God...
nor those due to him as man.

He had no home... was often hungry and thirsty...
was born in poverty... and died in final poverty.

I like to pretend to myself that I am poor in spirit.
But sometimes I find myself anxiously concerned about
trivialities –
I need a new freezer... a new TV... more gadgets for the
computer... new clothes... a new car...
I ought to take out another life insurance policy...
What sort of a pay rise can I expect, or ask for this time round?

I know well enough that I've got to work for my living, but I
wonder whether I'm often over-concerned about taking care for
tomorrow?

Help me, Lord Jesus, to be genuinely poor in spirit... to find a
proper balance between caution and recklessness... to deepen
my understanding of Providence.

THE ELEVENTH STATION
Jesus is nailed to the cross

Lamb of God

It is the sheer, unmitigated cruelty of it which disgusts us first of all. I seems unbelievable that human beings, created in the image and likeness of God, should be able to sink to such depths.

We call such acts barbaric, inhuman.

Cruelty survives today on the grand scale –
the concentration camps... genocide...
the senseless violence of today's crime...

the savage treatment by some of their children...
racism... torture... abuse... barbarism...

With me it may be a question of motes and beams. I am so
scandalised by the viciousness of some, that I scarcely notice the
speck of inhumanity in myself –

> my barbed wit...
> my lack of charity towards others on the roads...
> my disregard of those I don't want to like...
> my willingness to gossip and say something hurtful...
> my condescension towards those more ignorant than
>   I am...
>
> my impatience with those younger – or older – than
>   I am...

Pinpricks – which beside Christ's wounds are as nothing.
> But these are my faults,
> for which I am answerable.

Help me, Jesus, to heal the wounds caused by hate, and to show
to all people the love you have shown to me.

"Forgive us our trespasses
as we forgive those who trespass against us."

THE TWELFTH STATION

Jesus dies on the cross

Dying we live

"It was now about noon, and darkness came over the whole land until three in the afternoon, while the sun's light failed; and the curtain of the temple was torn in two.

Then Jesus, crying with a loud voice, said, 'Father, into your hands I commend my spirit.' Having said this, he breathed his last."

Luke 23:44-46

"He had no majesty that we should look at him,
nothing in his appearance that we should desire him.
He was despised and rejected by others;
a man of suffering and acquainted with infirmity;
But he was wounded for our transgressions,
crushed for our iniquities;
upon him was the punishment that made us whole,
and by his bruises we are healed."

Isaiah 53:2-6

"No one has greater love than this,
to lay down one's life for one's friends."

John 15:13

"I am the Lord, your God… your Saviour…
you are precious in my eyes… and I love you…"

see Isaiah 43:3-4

"Fear not, for I am with you…
you are my witnesses…
my chosen people…
the people whom I formed for myself…"

see 1 Peter 2:9

"Turn to me and be saved, for I am God…
Return to me, for I have redeemed you."

see Isaiah 44:22

"The Son of Man must be lifted up,
that whoever believes in him may have eternal life."

John 3:14-15

"Unless a grain of wheat falls into the earth and dies,
it remains just a single grain;
but if it dies, it bears much fruit."

John 12:24

THE THIRTEENTH STATION
Jesus is taken down from the cross

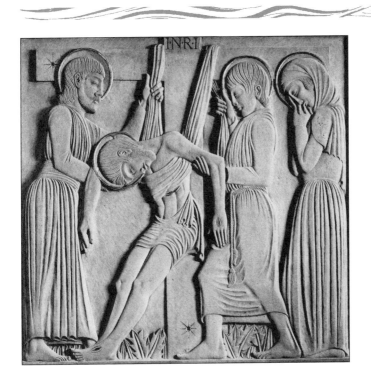

Emptiness

"We have one who in every respect has been tested as we are,
yet without sin."

Hebrews 4:15

The dead body of Jesus. It is hard to take this in… that Jesus
really died… that his body became a lifeless thing… an empty
shell.

If we have seen death we know how unreal a dead body looks.
It is so obviously empty... incomplete... utterly different from
what it was a few moments before.

And yet, "Truly this man was God's Son!"

Matthew 27:54

I wouldn't be human if I were entirely unafraid of death.

The saint may say, "My desire is to depart and to be with
    Christ";
but if I say this, the words are a little hollow.

Yet in spite of my natural human fear,
I have hope...
Christ has been there before me.

My only wish is that when God calls me
I shall be able to say, like Christ,
"It is finished, the work you gave me is done."

Help me, Lord Jesus, to approach death unafraid,
confident that I have tried to do your will.

The Fourteenth Station

Jesus is placed in the tomb and rises from the dead

VENIT·HORA·UT·CLARIFICETUR·FILIUS·HO—MINIS

AMEN·AMEN DICO·VOBIS NISI· GRA-NUM· FRU-MENTI· CAD-ENS·IN·TER-RAM·MORTU-UM·FUERIT IPSUM·SOLŪ MANET·SI AUTEM MORTUŪ FUERIT MULTUM FRUCTUM AFFERT

QVI·AMAT·ANIMAM·SUAM PERDET·EAM·ET·QVI·ODIT ANIMAM·SUAM· IN·HOC MUNDO·IN·VITAM·AETER-NAM·CUSTODIT·EAM

Resurrection!

"He descended into hell. The third day he rose again from the dead. He ascended into heaven and sits on the right hand of God the almighty Father…" continually interceding on our behalf.

The grave is only a passing resting place… for us as for Christ.

The life, death, resurrection and ascension of Jesus Christ is the promise for us of eternal life.

We are one body with Christ –
we are no longer alone in our pursuit of God...
we go with Christ...
we go as other Christs...

We share each other's blessings and burdens –
forgetful of self...
filled with the same hope...
fired with the same faith...
united in the same love for each other and for God.

I pray that in my life I may mirror Christ –
that I may truly die to sin...
that I may make my daily round my daily prayer...
that by my love I may lead others to Christ...
that in my God-given vocation I may learn to be all things to all
people.

I know that my Redeemer lives, and that
    through him,
    with him and
    in him,
    all of us shall find life.

An Examination of Conscience

EVERY now and then it is valuable for us to pause and look at ourselves, so as to see how we are living. It may be helpful to do this by reflecting on our Lord's teaching – for instance, the Beatitudes, one of the parables, or the account of the Last Judgement. Tradition suggests that the Portrait of Love given by St Paul (1 Corinthians 13:4-13) is a description of Jesus himself. So it is given here as a background against which we may see ourselves. If it is used as part of a night prayer, it may well be enough to choose just one phrase to ponder on.

"Love is patient, love is kind"...

Am I patient with myself?
Do I expect too much of myself?
Do I get angry with myself when I fail?

Am I impatient in prayer?
Do I stop praying if I don't get quick results?
Do I remember to pray for others?

Am I patient with others?
Do I get irritable at other people's failures or
weaknesses or eccentricities, or if they are less quick
or clever than I am?

Am I patient and kind with children, the elderly
and sick?
Am I patient with those who work with me or
for me?
Do I listen patiently to those in authority?

Am I gentle and kind in my speech?
Do I speak kindly and well of others?
Do I act kindly towards those who are in a less
privileged position than mine?

..."love is not envious, or boastful or arrogant..."

Am I envious of someone else's good fortune, or
success?
Do I try to keep up with my next-door neighbour?
Do I drive my children (or others) so that I can boast
of them?

Am I affronted if others don't live up to my
expectations?
Do I expect more of others than I do of myself?
Do I criticise others so that they lose confidence
in themselves?

Am I complacent about myself?
Am I hypocritical in the way I live?
Do I keep on comparing myself with others?

Do I look for praise from others?
Am I slow to thank, to encourage or to praise?
Do I bore others by talking about myself?

Do I bother to listen to others?
Am I slow to apologise or to admit my faults?
Do I show my gratitude to God and to my friends
for all they do for me?

..."love is not rude; it does not insist on its own way"...

Do I treat others with the respect due to them as
persons?
Am I chaste in my relationships with others?
Do I sin against purity in mind or action?

> Does my language reflect my human dignity?
> Am I ever arrogant, obstinate or overbearing?
> Does my attitude to others prevent them from
> speaking?

Do I insist on what I want before thinking about
others?
Do I inconvenience others by my selfish use of noisy
equipment?
Do I consider the effect that my actions will have on
others?

> Do I take a practical interest in the needs of the
> poorer parts of the world?
> Is my attitude to material things determined by
> selfish motives?
> Do I use my own or other people's property with
> due care?

Do I ever deliberately hurt another?
Do I seek for pleasure at the expense of others?
Does my selfishness ever lead me to ignore God?

..."love is not irritable or resentful"...

Am I touchy about my rights?
Am I prepared to accept criticism?
Do I feel slighted if others are preferred to me?

> How do I react to my failures?
> How do I respond if I am unjustly treated or
>   misunderstood?
> Am I willing to accept injustice as Christ did,
>   without complaining?

What is my attitude to law; do I ignore it if it
  inconveniences me?
Do I impose conditions on others that I am not
  prepared to accept myself?
Do I act on what Christ said, "If you love me you will
  keep my commandments"?

> Do I forgive those who sin against me?
> Do I ask forgiveness from those whom I have
>   sinned against?
> Am I resentful at the way God treats me?

Do I drive others to resentment by harshness, not
  listening, unreasonableness, thoughtlessness, or
  selfishness?
Am I depressed by my own weaknesses?
Do I resent my dependence on others and on God?

..."love rejoices in the truth"...

Am I a truthful person?
Do I try to grow in the understanding of truth?
Do I pray for God's Spirit of truth in my life?

> Do I repeat what I hear without bothering to
>   verify its truth or falsity?
> Do I gossip, or spread rumours, or scandal?
> Do I hide or distort truth by my speech, my
>   actions or my silence?

Do I respect those who sincerely hold beliefs different
    from mine?
Do I try to understand the beliefs of others?
Do I allow others freedom to accept truth, or do I put
    unfair pressures on them?

> Do I witness by word and example to the truth of
>   the Gospel?
> Do I take the trouble to learn more about God?
> Do I ever compromise the truth for fear of what
>   others may think?

Is my life a true reflection of my beliefs?
Do I try to share my vision of truth with others?
Do I look and listen for God in my life?

..."love bears all things, believes all things, hopes all things"...

Do I take Christ's advice: "Do not judge so that you may
   not be judged "?
                                                    Matthew 7:1
Am I quicker to judge others than I am to judge
   myself?
Do I try to understand why others do what they do?

   Do I make excuses for myself when I sin?
   Am I able to forgive myself?
   Do I have a firm hope that God will give me
      his grace?

Am I ready to accept others, whatever their faults?
Am I willing to trust others even when they let me
   down?
Do I help others to grow and to hope by putting my
   trust in them?

   Do I see justice and mercy as being in conflict?
   Am I rigid in my application of the law?
   Am I ready to be generous in forgiving?

Do I accept that I shall not be tried beyond my
   strength?
Do I believe that nothing can separate me from the
   love of God?
Am I able to accept my weaknesses, knowing that
   Christ's strength will work in me?

..."love endures all things"...

Do I grumble about the problems and hardships of my
    life – failure, sickness, unhappiness?
Do I accept that true love will always bring suffering?
Am I prepared to take up my cross daily and
    follow Christ?

> How do I try to face doubt?
> Do I try to overcome my own bad habits?
> Do I lose hope when it seems everyone is
>   against me?

Does my love for those close to me overcome their
    unkindnesses, their weaknesses, their letting me
    down, their failures?
Is my love for those who hurt me such that I can
    forgive them?

> Do I blame God for my sufferings, sicknesses and
>   difficulties?
> Is my love for God such that I can accept
>   persecution for speaking out in his name?
> Do I realise that to love another means to die
>   to self?

And, finally, do I accept that there are three things that
    last: faith, hope and love, and that the greatest of
    these is love?

A PRAYER OF SORROW

My God and Father,
I am deeply sorry for my sins.
When I have chosen wrong
and failed to do good,
I have turned from your love
and sinned against you.
I firmly intend, with your help,
to do penance,
to try not to sin,
and to avoid whatever leads me to sin.
Our Saviour Jesus Christ
suffered and died for us.
In his name, O God, have mercy,
and help me to love more generously.

THE ABSOLUTION

*In the Sacrament of Reconciliation the priest extends his
hands over the penitent's head, and says:*

God, the Father of mercies,
through the death and resurrection of his Son
has reconciled the world to himself
and sent the Holy Spirit among us
for the forgiveness of sins;
through the ministry of the Church
may God give you pardon and peace,
and I absolve you from your sins
in the name of the Father, and of the Son,
and of the Holy Spirit.
Amen.

Night Prayer

We end the day as we began it, by remembering God's presence.

In the name of the Father,
and of the Son,
and of the Holy Spirit. Amen.

Save us, Lord, while we are awake;
protect us while we sleep;
that we may keep watch with Christ
and rest with him in peace.

God has been with us throughout the day, but there may have been moments when we forgot his love and turned from him. We may pray for forgiveness:

TURN YOUR EAR, O Lord, and give answer
for I am poor and needy.
Preserve my life, for I am faithful:
save the servant who trusts in you.

You are my God, have mercy on me, Lord,
for I cry to you all day long.
Give joy to your servant, O Lord,
for to you I lift up my soul.

O Lord, you are good and forgiving,
full of love to all you call.
Give heed, O Lord, to my prayer
and attend to the sound of my voice.

In the day of distress I will call
and surely you will reply.   *Psalm 86:1-7*

He will always reply, but he asks us to know ourselves so that we may grow in holiness. Pause for a moment to see how you have lived today.

SOME PRAYERS OF SORROW

Lord God, our loving Father,
you know all my sins and failures,
my weaknesses and temptations.
I come to you with deep sorrow in my heart
for the wrong I have done and for the good I have
failed to do.
Forgive me, accept me, and strengthen me,
now and always. Amen.

———————

My God, I am sorry and ask forgiveness for my sins.
By the help of your grace I will try not to sin again.

There are many wonderful prayers of sorrow among the Psalms; see especially Psalm 51.

Despite any failures there may have been today, it will have been a day, like every day, marked by God's care and blessing. Remember quietly the good moments – the success, the happiness, the laughter, the peacefulness – and give thanks to God for them.

SOME PRAYERS OF THANKSGIVING

Lord, I thank you for all you have done for me today.
Help me to see you more clearly in my life.

———————

Remember, Lord, all those I love.
Teach me to be more generous towards them.

Stay close, Lord, to those who have been with me
today.
Comfort those whom I have harmed;
forgive those who may have hurt me;
bless those who have encouraged me.

May the work I have done today, Lord,
give glory to you
and be of service to my neighbour.

A PRAYER OF HAPPINESS AND PEACE

 PRESERVE ME, GOD, I take refuge in you.
I say to the Lord: 'You are my God.
My happiness lies in you alone.'

O Lord, it is you who are my portion and cup;
it is you yourself who are my prize.
The lot marked out for me is my delight:
welcome indeed the heritage that falls to me!

I will bless the Lord who gives me counsel,
who even at night directs my heart.
I keep the Lord ever in my sight;
since he is at my right hand, I shall stand firm.

And so my heart rejoices, my soul is glad;
even my body shall rest in safety.
You will show me the path of life,
the fullness of joy in your presence,
at your right hand, happiness for ever.

from Psalm 16

A PRAYER FOR PEACE

 May the Lord support us all the day long,
till the shades lengthen and the evening comes,
and the busy world is hushed,
and the fever of life is over,
and our work is done.
Then in his mercy
may he give us a safe lodging,
and a holy rest,
and peace at the last. Amen.

Cardinal Newman

*As we end the day we can remember again that we belong to
the whole family of the saints, and ask Mary, our mother, to
pray for us:*

 Hail, Holy Queen, Mother of Mercy!
Hail our life, our sweetness and our hope.
To you do we cry, poor banished children of Eve;
to you do we send up our sighs,
mourning and weeping in this vale of tears.
Turn, then, most gracious advocate,
your eyes of mercy towards us;
and after this our exile,
show unto us the blessed fruit of your womb, Jesus.
O clement, O loving, O sweet Virgin Mary.

 May the Lord grant me a quiet night,
and a perfect end.
Amen.

Index

Included in this index are the titles of the principal headings (with the page numbers printed in italic), a selection of ideas and themes (sometimes suggested by a single word in the quotation), and a separate list of Authors and Sources quoted in the first part of the prayer book.

Absolution 190
Agony 112
Agony in the Garden, The *111–113*
Anger 28-29, 164
Annunciation, The *100–102*
Anxiety 33, 101
Apostles' Creed, The 45
Ascension, The *123–125*
Asking 32, 33
Assumption, The *127–129*
Baptism 118
Beatitudes, The *133–151*
Birth of Our Lord, The *104–106*
Blessing *91–92*
Boastfulness 184
Breaking point *167–168*
Burden 90, *117–118*, 146, 157
Carrying of the Cross, The *117–118*
Cheerful giver 27
Childlike 35, 67
Children of God 87
Church, The *84–85*
Collapse *171–172*
Comfort 138, 193
Compassion 49, 93, 139, 165
Condemnation 155
Confidence, A Prayer of 13
Conscience, Examination of 183
Conversion *66–67*
Courage 146

Creation 39, 61, 69, *81–82*
Cross, The Way of the *153–182*
Cross-bearing 146, *157–158*
Crowning with Thorns, The *115–116*
Crucifixion, The *119–120*
Day's Work, The 13, *36–38*
Death 62–65, 98, *117–120, 177–178*, 180
Desolation *161–162*
Dignity 36, 185
Discipleship *19–21*
Dying we live *177–178*
Emptiness *179–180*
Encouragement 59, 184
Eternal life 147, 181
Examination of Conscience, An *183–190*
Faith *43–45*
Falling *159–160*
Family *34–36*
Fear 138, 158
Finding in the Temple, The *109–110*
'Follow me' 20, 25, 26, 117
Forgiveness 30, *48–51*, 166, 186
Freedom *86–88*
Gifts of the Holy Spirit 60
Giving *26–27*
Grace 60, 80, 129
Growth *70–71*
Healing *51–52*
Holiness, A Longing for 96
Holy Spirit, The Coming of the *125–127*
Hope *72–73*, 182
Humble of heart *140–141*
Humility 22, 25, 35, *46–48*, 60
Journey's End 98
Joy *56–57*
Jubilee *89–98*
Judging others 156, 188
Justice *52–54*, 142

Kindness 22, 49, 53, 92, 127
Labour *36–38*
Lamb of God *175–176*
Law *58–59*
Leadership *22*
Light 45, 85, 107
'Light of the world' 21, 54, 107
Lord is my Shepherd, The 13
Lord's Prayer, The 12
Lost and found *92–93*
Love 58, 70, *74–77*, *183–189*
Magnificat, The 47
Meekness *140–141*
Mercy *144–145*
Millennium, The *90, 91*
Mourning *138–139*
Mustard seed 43, 84
Naked *173–174*
New heart, A 42
Obedience 27
Our Father, The 12
Our Lady, Queen of Heaven *129–131*
Pain 114
Parents 35
Patience *67–69*, 183
Peace *54–56*, *148–149*, 193, 194
Perfect 133
Persecution 34, 72, 90, *150–151*
Perseverance 86, 168
Petition *32–33*
Poor in Spirit *136–138*
Poverty 26, *136–137*
Praise and Thanksgiving 11, *82–84*, 192
Prayer 11, *31-33*, 191
Presence of God, The *77–80*
Presentation, The *107–108*
Pride 46, 160
Pure in heart *146–147*

Reconciliation *92–93*, 190
Renewal *96–98*
Repentance 66
Resurrection, The 43, 65, *121–123*, *181–182*, 190
Revenge 23, 48
Righteousness 52, *142–148*, 150
Rudeness 185
Saviour 105, 178, 190
Scourging at the Pillar, The *113–115*
Seeking God 31, 32, 66
Self-denial 25
Self-giving, A Prayer of 13
Service *23–24*
Sharing *94–95*, *163–164*
Sign of the Cross, The 11
Simon of Cyrene 117, 163
Sorrow 30, 31, 190, 192
Spirit *42–43*, *125–127*
Stations of the Cross, The *153–182*
Suffering *69–70*, 90
Thanksgiving *95–96*, 192
Treasure in heaven 26
Truth 187
Unity *59–60*
Visitation, The *102–104*
Vocation 18, 102, 182
Wakefulness 32
Way of the Cross, The *153–182*
Weakness 34, 76, 79, 93, 94, 155, 160
Weep not *169–170*
Witness 106, 114, 124
Women of Jerusalem, The 169
Work *36–38*
Worry 33, 53, 63
Youth 18, 46